D0485710

THE CHOSEN

Chaim Potok

Copyright © 2002 by SparkNotes LLC

All rights reserved. No part of this book may be used or reproduced in any manner whatsoever without the written permission of the Publisher.

SPARKNOTES is a registered trademark of SparkNotes LLC

This edition published by Spark Publishing

Spark Publishing
A Division of SparkNotes LLC
120 Fifth Avenue, 8th Floor
New York, NY 10011

Any book purchased without a cover is stolen property, reported as "unsold and destroyed" to the Publisher, who receives no payment for such "stripped books."

Please submit all comments and questions or report errors to www.sparknotes.com/errors

Printed and bound in the United States

ISBN 1-58663-504-2

Introduction:
Stopping to Buy SparkNotes on a Snowy Evening

Whose words these are you *think* you know.
Your paper's due tomorrow, though;
We're glad to see you stopping here
To get some help before you go.

Lost your course? You'll find it here.
Face tests and essays without fear.
Between the words, good grades at stake:
Get great results throughout the year.

Once school bells caused your heart to quake
As teachers circled each mistake.
Use SparkNotes and no longer weep,
Ace every single test you take.

Yes, books are lovely, dark, and deep,
But only what you grasp you keep,
With hours to go before you sleep,
With hours to go before you sleep.

CONTENTS

CONTEXT

CHAIM POTOK, AN AMERICAN rabbi and scholar, was born into an Orthodox Jewish family in 1929. The eldest son of Polish immigrants, Potok grew up in New York City and started writing fiction when he was only sixteen years old. Potok received a rigorous religious and secular education at Yeshiva University, a school very similar to the fictional Hirsch Seminary and College in *The Chosen*. He then received his rabbinic ordination from the Jewish Theological Seminary and a Ph.D. in philosophy from the University of Pennsylvania. He died on July 23, 2002 at his home in Pennsylvania.

Potok wrote numerous novels, plays, and short stories, and was a painter all his life. As an author, Potok is best known for exploring the interplay between religious Judaism and the broader secular world, a fundamental tension in his own life.

The Chosen, Potok's first novel, is part of a larger tradition of twentieth-century Jewish-American literature, which includes the authors Abraham Cahan, Henry Roth, Bernard Malamud, Saul Bellow, Philip Roth, and Cynthia Ozick. The tensions between tradition and modern American life is a frequent theme in Jewish literature and, more broadly, in American immigrant literature. *The Chosen* explores this theme in an unusual and distinctive manner, focusing on the ways in which different Jewish communities attempt to strike a balance between tradition and modernity, and the tension this effort creates. Instead of becoming completely assimilated into American culture, Potok's characters try to balance their religious interests with their secular ones.

The Chosen's two central characters are a Hasid and a traditional Orthodox Jew. The Hasidim are known for their mystical interpretation of Judaism and for their faithful devotion to their leaders. In contrast, traditional Orthodoxy emphasizes a rational and intellectual approach to Judaism. The novel examines Jewish identity from within these contexts by telling the parallel stories of two Jewish adolescents who are similar enough to become best friends, yet different enough to change each other's view of the world.

Like many of Potok's novels, *The Chosen* takes place at a significant moment in world history. The first third of the novel unfolds during the Allied offensive in World War II, the middle third deals with the American Jewish community's response to the Holocaust, and the final third is concerned with the Zionist movement to create a Jewish state in Palestine. These events are not merely backdrop for the novel, but contribute significantly to its plot and thematic content. For example, the differing ways Reb Saunders and David Malter react to the Holocaust indicate a major difference between them. Reb Saunders's argues that the murder of six million Jews is God's will and that, in response, man can only wait for God to bring the Messiah. In contrast, David Malter believes that American Jews must give the Holocaust meaning by preserving Jewish culture in America and by creating a homeland in Palestine. This fundamental difference of opinion between the two men eventually has important consequences for the novel's plot.

In tracing the friendship of two religious adolescent boys influenced by their fathers, Potok offers insight into the challenges of faith facing the American Jewish community in the wake of the Holocaust. Moreover, the book's historical backdrop catalyzes one of the novel's central conflicts: the conflict between tradition and modernity. Throughout the novel, characters are forced to choose between isolating themselves from the outside world and retreating into tradition—as Reb Saunders advocates—or actively embracing issues that extend beyond a single community—as demonstrated by David Malter's activism. Among other subjects, the novel studies the different ways of balancing Jewish observance with life in twentieth-century America.

PLOT OVERVIEW

THE CHOSEN traces a friendship between two Jewish boys growing up in Brooklyn at the end of World War II. Reuven Malter, the narrator and one of the novel's two protagonists, is a traditional Orthodox Jew. He is the son of David Malter, a dedicated scholar and humanitarian. Danny Saunders, the other protagonist, is a brilliant Hasid with a photographic memory and a passion for psychoanalysis. Danny is the son of Reb Saunders, the pious and revered head of a great Hasidic dynasty. Over the course of eighteen chapters (divided into three books), the novel tells the story of the friendship that develops between the two boys, and it examines the tensions that arise as their cultures collide with each other and with modern American society.

In Book One, Reuven's high school softball team plays against Danny's yeshiva team in a Sunday game. Tension quickly develops as the Hasidic team insults the faith of Reuven and his teammates. The game becomes a kind of holy war for both teams, and the resulting competition is fierce. In the final inning, Reuven is pitching. Danny smacks a line drive at Reuven that hits him in the eye, shattering his glasses and nearly blinding him. Reuven is rushed to the hospital, where he spends a week recuperating. While in the hospital, he becomes friendly with two fellow patients: Tony Savo, an exboxer, and Billy Merrit, a young blind boy.

Danny visits Reuven in the hospital to ask his forgiveness, and a tenuous friendship begins. Tentatively, the two boys begin talking about their intellectual interests and their hopes for the future. Danny reveals that he has an astounding intellect, including a photographic memory, and he displays a prodigious knowledge of the Talmud. Danny also confides that he secretly reads every day in the public library, studying books of which his father would disapprove. He also says that a nice older man often recommends books to him. Both boys are surprised to discover that David Malter—Reuven's father—is this man.

Book Two focuses on the rest of Reuven and Danny's time in high school. Reuven begins spending Shabbat afternoons at Danny's house. On their first Sabbath together, Danny introduces Reuven to his father, Rabbi Isaac Saunders. Reuven witnesses a strange ritual:

Reb Saunders quizzes Danny in public during their congregation's Sabbath meal. Reb Saunders also surprises Reuven, asking him a question about the speech Reb Saunders gave. Reuven answers correctly, impressing Reb Saunders.

Danny and Reuven begin spending most afternoons together in the library and Saturdays studying Talmud with Reb Saunders. Reuven learns that Reb Saunders believes in raising his son in silence. Except for discussions of Talmud, Danny's father never speaks to him directly, though he begins to use Reuven as an indirect means of talking to his son. Outside of the shul, Danny and Reuven spend almost all their free time together and have many conversations.

Meanwhile, almost everyone is obsessed with news about World War II. President Roosevelt's death in April 1945 saddens the entire country. In May, Reuven and his father celebrate the end of the war in Europe, but are shocked by the discovery of concentration camps behind enemy lines. Everyone, even Reb Saunders, is disturbed by the reports of Jewish suffering and death at the hands of the Nazis.

After Reuven's finals that spring, his father suffers a heart attack, and Reuven goes to live with the Saunders family for the summer. While there, Danny and Reuven talk a great deal, and Reuven learns that Danny plans to study Freudian psychoanalysis instead of inheriting his father's position in the Hasidic community. Danny hopes that his younger brother Levi can succeed his father in his place. In the fall, both boys begin studying at Hirsch College in Brooklyn.

Book Three chronicles the experiences of Reuven and Danny at Samson Raphael Hirsch Seminary and College. Danny immediately becomes a leader of the Hasidic student body, but he is disappointed by the college's emphasis on experimental, rather than Freudian, psychology. Meanwhile, Reuven decides that he is firmly committed to becoming a rabbi. Reuven is also worried about his father, whose health is rapidly deteriorating in part due to his frenetic Zionist activity. In school, Danny continues to be frustrated by the psychology curriculum, but Reuven convinces Danny to discuss his differences with his psychology professor, and the resulting conversation is very productive for Danny. With the help of Reuven's tutelage in mathematics, Danny comes to appreciate the value of the experimental method.

As the conflicts over a Jewish state become more intense, tensions swell among the various student factions at the college. After David Malter gives a highly publicized pro-Zionist speech at Madison Square Garden, Reb Saunders, who is staunchly anti-Zionist, forbids Danny from speaking to Reuven. The silence between the two boys continues into their second year at college. They both take Rav Gershenson's Talmud class, which allows them to interact indirectly. Yet Reuven misses Danny's friendship terribly, especially after Reuven's father suffers a second heart attack. As David Malter recovers, Reuven rigorously studies the Talmud and dazzles the entire class—including Danny—with one particularly brilliant classroom display of knowledge. After Reuven's father returns from the hospital, the college is staggered by the news that an alumnus of Hirsch died in the fighting in Israel. Finally, during Reuven and Danny's third year of college, after the United Nations officially declares the creation of the State of Israel and after it becomes clear that Israel will triumph in its battles against the Arabs, Reb Saunders relents and allows the two boys to speak to each other again.

Danny and Reuven quickly resume their intense friendship. Over the summer, Reuven returns to Danny's shul, goes to Danny's sister's wedding, and sees Reb Saunders again. Reuven still harbors anger toward Danny's father, and ignores the older man's invitation to a Sabbath Talmud discussion. During the boys' final year at college, Reuven sees Reb Saunders while attending Danny's brother's Bar Mitzvah, and again the rabbi invites Reuven over. Reuven ignores the request.

Meanwhile, Danny secretly applies to graduate programs in psychology, but soon realizes that his father will inevitably see letters from the schools in the family's mailbox. One night, after a discussion with his father, Reuven realizes that Reb Saunders is asking him to come over so he can indirectly talk to Danny. Reuven goes to their house, and Reb Saunders, using Reuven as a buffer to speak to Danny, finally explains why he raised Danny in silence. He says he always knew his son had a great mind, but was worried that his soul was empty, unable to empathize with the suffering of others. Silence was a way to make Danny explore his own soul and feel the suffering of the world. Reb Saunders further reveals that he is aware of Danny's plan to become a psychologist instead of a rabbi. He apologizes to Reuven for separating the two boys, and he apologizes to Danny for raising him in silence. At the same time, he says he saw no other way to raise Danny to become a true tzaddik—a tzaddik for the world, not only a tzaddik for his congregation. Later, in front of his congregation, he gives his blessing to Danny and the life he has chosen for himself. Danny shaves his beard and earlocks, and enrolls in a graduate program at Columbia University.

CHARACTER LIST

Reuven Malter The narrator of the novel and one of its two
protagonists. Reuven is a traditional Orthodox Jew
who lives with his father in a brownstone apartment in
Brooklyn. He observes the Ten Commandments and
attends a Jewish parochial school, or yeshiva, where his
father teaches. He is an intelligent, conscientious, and
popular boy, talented in softball, math, and Talmud
study. *The Chosen* is primarily the story of his long and
sometimes complicated friendship with Danny
Saunders. As Reuven and Danny struggle toward
adulthood during the tumultuous end of World War II
and creation of the modern State of Israel, Reuven
examines his understanding of religion, culture, and
spirituality.

Danny Saunders The novel's other protagonist. Danny is the son
of Reb Saunders and heir apparent to his father's
Hasidic dynasty. He is a brilliant scholar with a
photographic memory and a deep interest in Freud and
psychoanalysis. Danny attends his father's Hasidic
yeshiva, but he reads secular books in secret at the
public library. He is torn between his duty to his father
and his own ideas about how to live his life. As the heir
to a Hasidic dynasty, he feels an obligation to remain
within his cloistered, extremely conservative Jewish
community. At the same time, he longs to study
intellectual ideas in the outside world.

David Malter A traditional Orthodox Jew and a teacher, scholar,
writer, and humanitarian. Mr. Malter raises his son,
Reuven, to be an ethical, caring, and intellectually
honest young man, well-versed in both Judaic and
secular studies. Mr. Malter is notorious within the
Hasidic community for his controversial Biblical
scholarship and his outspoken support of Zionism. His
health deteriorates as the novel progresses due to his
tireless hard work on behalf of the Zionist movement.

CHARACTER LIST

He wants Reuven to become a mathematics professor, but once he realizes his son is dedicated to becoming a rabbi, he fully supports Reuven's decision. Throughout the book, he encourages the intellectual curiosity of both his son and Danny Saunders.

Reb Isaac Saunders The pious and zealous patriarch of a Hasidic dynasty. Reb Saunders's home is also the center of study and prayer for his followers, who join him at his table every Shabbat. Reb Saunders is a wise, learned, and deeply religious sage who raises Danny in silence, speaking to him only when discussing the Talmud. At the end of the novel, he reveals that he raised Danny in silence in order to teach him to have compassion for others. Reb Saunders is fervently committed to his strict and limited Hasidic worldview, and he imposes his views on everyone around him.

Levi Saunders Danny's sickly younger brother. Unlike Danny, Levi is not raised in silence. Danny hopes that Levi will take over his father's dynasty so that Danny can study psychology instead.

Mr. Galanter The gym instructor at Reuven's yeshiva. Mr. Galanter leads Reuven's high school softball team and brings Reuven to the hospital after his eye injury. He speaks to his team using military metaphors, and the boys wonder why he is not fighting in World War II. Mr. Galanter later tells Reuven that he "couldn't make it as a soldier," but he never elaborates.

Rav Gershenson An Orthodox rabbi and Danny and Reuven's teacher in the highest-level Talmud class at the Hirsch Seminary and College. To Reuven's surprise, Rav Gershenson is familiar with David Malter's Talmudic criticism, and he considers Mr. Malter a great scholar.

Professor Nathan Appleman The chairman of the psychology department at the Hirsch Seminary and College. Professor Appleman's class frustrates Danny at first, because Appleman critiques Freud's methods and focuses on experimental psychology. However, after Danny and Appleman discuss their differences, Danny comes to respect Appleman and his methodology.

Manya The loving Russian housekeeper who cooks and cleans the Malters' apartment.

Tony Savo A patient who occupies one of the hospital beds next to Reuven. Tony Savo's speech, which he peppers with boxing terms, reflects his former career as a professional prizefighter. Reuven and Mr. Savo become friends, and he warns Reuven to beware of religious fanatics like Danny. Mr. Savo had to have his right eye surgically removed.

Billy Merrit A young boy who sleeps in the hospital bed on the opposite side of Reuven from Mr. Savo. Billy became blind after a car accident and is in the hospital in preparation for an operation to restore his sight. Reuven later learns that the operation is unsuccessful.

Roger Merrit Billy Merrit's father. He was the driver in the car accident that resulted in his wife's death and Billy's blindness.

Dr. Snydman The doctor who operates on Reuven's eye at Brooklyn Memorial Hospital.

Mickey A sickly six-year-old boy Reuven meets while in Brooklyn Memorial Hospital. Mickey has lived most of his life in the hospital due to a strange stomach condition.

Sidney Goldberg Reuven's friend and softball teammate. Sidney is a likeable and athletic boy.

Davey Cantor Reuven's timid friend and softball teammate. At Hirsch College, Davey is the student who informs Reuven about FDR's death.

Dov Shlomowitz Danny's burly Hasidic classmate and softball teammate.

Mrs. Carpenter A kindly yet strict nurse at Brooklyn Memorial Hospital.

Solomon Maimon A young Polish Jew who lived in the second half of the eighteenth century. Solomon Maimon was a ravenously intelligent student who studied non-Jewish literature after the Talmud could not satisfy his hunger for knowledge. As a result of his heresy, he died rootless and alone. In Chapter 6, David Malter says that Danny Saunders reminds him of Solomon Maimon.

ANALYSIS OF MAJOR CHARACTERS

REUVEN MALTER

Potok chooses Reuven to narrate *The Chosen*, even though the novel's central conflict is Danny's desire to break away from his obligation to inherit his father's position as Tzaddik. Reuven works well as a narrator because we share his position as a curious outsider looking in on the unfamiliar, secret world of Hasidism. Reuven is a more accessible character than Danny; it is more difficult for us to relate to Danny's unique genius and his Hasidic lifestyle. At the same time, these aspects of Danny's character make him very interesting, and as narrator, Reuven is able to instill in us the same fascination with Danny that Reuven himself feels.

Reuven's presence also reminds us that *The Chosen* is not just the story of Danny's struggle between his obligation to the traditions of his family and the possibilities of a modern, secular society. Reuven also deals with conflicts and change. Through his interactions with Danny and Reb Saunders, his perspective on the world is broadened. He deepens his empathy for others and enlarges his intellect. Both Reuven and Danny are protagonists, and each is central to developing the novel's themes and driving its plot. Potok's focus on two protagonists instead of one underscores the importance of friendships and relationships to the novel, and the related ideas of reciprocity, choice, and compromise.

DANNY SAUNDERS

Although *The Chosen* focuses equally on both Reuven's and Danny's personal and religious development, it is Danny's story that provides the central conflict of the novel and sets in motion both protagonists' process of discovery. Danny and Reuven's similarities—their love of learning, quick minds, and deep Jewish faith—allow them to relate to one another and become friends. At the same time, their differences in family situations, culture, and relationships to the non-Jewish secular world allow them to learn from one another. Throughout the novel, Danny learns restraint and introspection from Reuven. As Reb Saunders points out in the final chapter, Reuven entered Danny's life when Danny "was ready to rebel." Reb Saunders argues that God sent Reuven to Danny to help him.

At the beginning of the novel, Danny is tense and unsure about how to deal with his inner desire to rebel against his upbringing. He has difficulty speaking openly, and only after warming up to Reuven does he reveal the awkwardness of his situation. Furthermore, Danny's repressed anger toward his father has made him highly susceptible to embracing any criticism of Hasidism. In Chapter 8, Danny reads Graetz's *History of the Jews*. The book contains a harsh denunciation of the Hasidim, but Danny reads it with a surprising lack of skepticism. Reuven, on the other hand, provides a tempering, rational perspective, balancing Danny's anger and frustration with compassion and contemplation. By the end of the novel, Danny has resolved his conflict with his father; furthermore, like Reuven, he has developed a broadened, more balanced sense of himself and the world around him.

Sanford Sternlicht writes that the conflict between Danny and his father should be seen in terms of Freud's theory of the Oedipus complex, which posits that a son holds an unconscious wish to take his father's place and be the sole object of his mother's affection. Sternlicht argues that Danny expresses his hostility toward his father as aversion to the idea of taking his father's place as leader of the congregation. Sternlicht adds, "Most significantly, it is Danny's reading of Freud that provides much of the ammunition for his successful revolt against and defeat of his father, who, unconsciously, may be trying to deprive Danny of his individual manhood by turning him into a clone of himself." Yet Danny's rebellion is against his culture as well as his father. He has a repressed need to rebel against the traditional, constrictive role of a tzaddik—and the type of life that Danny fears his father wants him to lead.

DAVID MALTER

In an interview presented in Edward Abramson's book *Chaim Potok*, Potok says that a "teacher should be somebody like Reuven Malter's father. In many ways he exemplifies the Jewish adventure." David Malter represents the ideal American Jewish father. He combines religious rigor with scientific inquiry and a love of knowledge, all of which he tempers with his overwhelming love and respect for his son. Throughout the book, David Malter displays a profound tolerance of and respect for a variety of traditions. His open-minded spiritual and intellectual rigor represents the balanced perspective that both boys want to achieve. He is an individual who understands the importance of relationships and reciprocity, and he values and accepts the dual perspectives of tradition and secularism. David Malter's perfection makes him the novel's most one-dimensional, static character, but his character does evolve in one crucial way. After he learns about the Holocaust, we see him change from a gentle, mellow father into an impassioned Zionist activist. David Malter states his motivations for his ceaseless Zionist activity clearly in Chapter 13, when he explains to Reuven that a "man must fill his life with meaning, meaning is not automatically given to life." This statement reflects David Malter's growing feeling that it is not enough to wait passively for biblical prophesy, as Reb Saunders does. Rather, David Malter feels it is up to mankind to actively give meaning to the world and make sense of the horrible suffering of the Holocaust. As Sternlicht explains, the only way for David Malter to make sense of the Holocaust is for the Holocaust to incite the Jewish people's return to the ancient land of Israel. Unlike Reb Saunders, David Malter believes that religion should impact politics, and that it is important for Jews to actively engage the outside world.

REB SAUNDERS

For most of the novel, Reb Saunders is an extraordinarily limited character, who embodies the stereotypes of the intolerant religious fanatic and of the provincial immigrant father. Reb Saunders's harsh public quizzes, his refusal to speak to his son, his explosion toward Reuven concerning Zionism, and his prohibition of Danny and Reuven's friendship all contribute to our impression of him as a fierce, autocratic, and narrow-minded individual. We assume that his only concern for Danny is that he study obsessively and follow the traditions, rituals, and customs of Hasidic Judaism, in preparation to inherit his father's position as Tzaddik of his congregation.

Yet a few of Reuven's early observations subtly contradict this impression. The first occurs during Danny's heated Talmud battles with his father, when Reuven observes that losing to Danny makes Reb Saunders happier than winning. Reb Saunders's happy willingness to have his son disprove his arguments suggests a passionate, caring, and respectful love for his son that does not fit with the rest of his behavior. Later during the same Talmud session, Reb Saunders confronts Reuven and reveals that he knows about Danny's library visits, but he expresses no anger. Instead, he seems saddened and, above all, bewildered. This reaction to Danny's treachery is not what Reuven, Danny, or we were expecting. Finally, Reb Saunders's suffering manner—the way he walks as if he is carrying a burden, the way he suddenly bursts into tears—seems to indicate a mysterious level of compassion and empathy.

In *The Chosen*'s final chapter, Reb Saunders finally reveals the motives behind his harsh actions, showing us he is a complex, conflicted character. Reb Saunders seems to have a limited, parochial perspective, but, in fact, it is Reuven's view of Reb Saunders that is limited. To everyone's surprise, Reb Saunders is not enraged that Danny has decided not to become a rabbi, and he reveals he has known of Danny's feelings for quite a while. He explains that his silence toward Danny, which Reuven assumes reflects a lack of love, reflects just the opposite. He sees his silence as a selfless act to give his son emotion and compassion, respect and empathy for others, and an awareness of the suffering of others.

However, despite Reb Saunder's explanation of his cruel actions, his method is nevertheless dubious. Even Reb Saunders himself acknowledges the pain he caused, revealing his own conflicted feelings about the Hasidic tradition. We get the sense that he struggled to find another way to teach his son, but failed—he had no choice but to teach through silence. In the end, Reb Saunders is a very complex character. He represents the dangers of fanaticism and harmful isolationist behavior, but he also shows a profound, painful love for Danny and a deeply human sense of the importance of empathy and emotion.

THEMES, MOTIFS & SYMBOLS

THEMES

Themes are the fundamental and often universal ideas explored in a literary work.

THE IMPORTANCE OF PARALLELS

The Chosen is a bildungsroman, a novel that traces the intellectual, moral, and psychological growth of a young protagonist. What makes *The Chosen* unusual is its focus on the development of two main characters rather than one. As a result of their friendship, Reuven and Danny develop along parallel lines. To reinforce the importance of Reuven and Danny's relationship to their respective developments, Potok fills his novel with a seemingly endless array of pairs, parallels, complements, and contrasts. Some characters' parallel relationships are important because they fulfill similar roles. For example, David Malter and Rav Gershenson parallel each other because in David Malter's absence, Rav Gershenson becomes Reuven's wise instructor. Other parallel characters are important because they complement one another by sharing knowledge. Reuven and Danny are one such pair: Danny introduces Reuven to his broad yet rigorous method of analyzing Talmud, while Reuven teaches Danny patience and open-mindedness when Danny is frustrated with experimental psychology. Still other parallel characters are important because they contrast with one another. For example, while David Malter and Reb Saunders are both fathers and religious scholars, they demonstrate fundamentally different beliefs about parenting and religious tolerance.

In addition to creating parallel characters, Potok pairs abstract concepts as well. He relates Reuven's experience with near-blindness to Danny's experience with silence. He points out the similarity between Danny and Reuven's apartments. He even connects events, such as David Malter's heart attack after FDR's death.

On one level, the use of parallels makes us aware of how important relationships are in Potok's world. Potok argues that every person, every object, everything in his the universe is intimately connected to something else. For Potok, there can be no growth, no development, and no progress without an awareness of this ever-present connection.

On a deeper level, Potok's pairs echo the psychoanalytic theory of Jacques Lacan. Lacan was a French psychoanalyst and student of Freud's works. His most famous contribution to psychology was his formulation of what he called the mirror stage. According to Lacan, there is a crucial stage in human development when, as infants, we first see ourselves in a mirror. This marks the first time in our lives, Lacan explains, when our interior sense of ourselves is associated with an external image of ourselves. It is a moment of important identification, when we begin to develop a sense of our own identity. Lacan argues that we need external images, reflections of ourselves, to define our sense of who we are. The parallels in *The Chosen* are structured in this way. The complements and contrasts in the world are mirrors the characters use to develop their sense of the world and themselves.

SILENCE AS A PATH TO THE SOUL

Chaim Potok's working title for *The Chosen* was *A Time For Silence*. Silence is present throughout the novel, although its importance is obscure until the novel's resolution. Potok often inserts the word "silence" in the text, leaving us to figure out its meaning. For example, in Chapter 4, Reuven notes that a "warm silence, ... not in the least bit awkward" passes between him and Danny. At first glance, this use of the word "silence" seems unrelated to the mysterious silence between Danny and his father. But later, we learn that silence, like communication, can help people better understand each other.

Reb Saunders reveals his reasons for his silence toward Danny in Chapter 18. By depriving Danny of a certain physical stimulus, Reb Saunders forces him to cultivate other senses of perception. In other words, the imposed silence forces Danny to mature. Danny's experience with silence parallels Reuven's experience with blindness, forcing him to turn inward, and thus develop a better sense of his soul, a greater empathy for others, and a better sense of the world and his role in it.

Yet Potok does not completely endorse Reb Saunder's treatment of Danny. When Reuven meets Danny, he is not accustomed to silence. Reuven's relationship with his father is based on a constant, easy flow of conversation; as a friend, Mr. Malter is a good listener and offers sound advice. As a result, Reuven thinks of silence as something strange, dark, and empty, and he considers Reb Saunders's silence toward Danny inexplicable and cruel. At the end of the novel, after Reb Saunders explains his silence, Reuven and his father continue to wonder whether its benefits outweigh its drawbacks.

Silence is alternately frightening, confusing, warm, and welcome, but it always leads to introspection, allowing the characters' humanity, spirituality, and empathy for others to grow. Reuven is blind to moments when silence is comfortable, warm, and inviting, but Potok is careful to show that silence is not always harmful, despite Reuven's initial ignorance of its nuances. Silence occurs between every pair of major characters at some point in the novel. Danny and his father are the most prominent example, but silence exists also between David Malter and Reb Saunders, who never speak to each other in the novel. Danny and David Malter do not speak after their encounter in the hospital until the very end of the book; Reuven and Danny have silence imposed upon their friendship by Reb Saunders; David Malter imposes a kind of silence on Reuven by refusing to explain Reb Saunders's way of raising Danny; and Reuven imposes a silence on Reb Saunders when he ignores the rebbe's requests for conversation. Again, Potok shows that silence exists everywhere, in many forms, and has as much meaning in a relationship as words.

THE CONFLICT BETWEEN TRADITION AND MODERNITY

Though Potok disagrees, many critics believe the conflict between Hasidic tradition and American secular modernity is the central theme of *The Chosen*. Much of Jewish-American literature focuses on the tension between traditional Jewish values and modern American mores, and *The Chosen* can be read as part of that tradition. What is unusual about the novel is how little we see of the world beyond Danny and Reuven's Jewish community in Brooklyn—even the hospital keeps kosher. We never see any of the characters interacting directly with the outside world. Even when David Malter speaks at Madison Square Garden for the first time, Reuven does not attend, making the event seem far away and reinforcing Reuven's distance from the world beyond his Jewish community.

Instead of coming from the world outside Reuven and Danny's neighborhood, the tension in the novel is between two conflicting philosophies within the Jewish community: Reb Saunders's isolationist fanaticism and David Malter's more open-minded awareness of the world around him. Reb Saunders's traditionalist mindset is stubborn and parochial. For most of the novel, he is unwilling to engage the outside world or interpret Judaism in ways other than his own. David Malter, on the other hand, remains tolerant of other points of view, even Reb Saunders's. Most important, David Malter is willing to adapt his religious beliefs to engage modernity constructively. With his activism and scientific approach to Talmudic study, David Malter represents Potok's ideal of the modern American Jew. He manages to fuse a traditional sense of devotion and spirituality with a commitment to the larger world around him.

At the end of the novel, Reb Saunders says that he wants Danny to be a "tzaddik for the world." With this acknowledgement of Danny's responsibilities to the world as a whole, we get a sense that Reb Saunders's fanaticism has evolved into a more open-minded expression of religion and spirituality.

CHOOSING VERSUS BEING CHOSEN

According to tradition, Jews are the "chosen people," somehow set apart from the rest of the world, especially in terms of their obligation to God. None of the novel's characters actively chooses to be Jewish; it is an aspect of each character's life that has been chosen for him by virtue of his birth. Each of the characters in the novel, though he loves his religion and does not resent it, struggles with what it means to be chosen in this way. For Reb Saunders, being Jewish means one must accept a special set of obligations to study Torah and serve God. For David Malter, being Jewish means a certain intellectual and spiritual obligation to fill one's life with meaning. For Reuven, being Jewish means a joyful commitment to religious tradition and intellectual engagement. For Danny, being Jewish means carrying a difficult burden at the same time as it means respecting a proud intellectual tradition.

However, though Danny enjoys the Jewish tradition, the obligations he has as a result of his family's Hasidic culture encumber him greatly. Like his religion, Danny's culture and its values were not something Danny chose, but something chosen for him. By virtue of his status as first-born male, he is chosen to inherit his father's position. Perhaps in another time and place, this obligation would not so upset Danny. But, as Reb Saunders himself acknowledges in *The Chosen*'s final chapter, modern America is a land of opportunity and choices. As an American, Danny does not have to passively accept the destiny that was chosen for him; he can actively choose what he wants to do with his life. Therefore, even though Danny does not rebel against his religion, the conflict between Danny and his father is a conflict between accepting what has been chosen and choosing one's own path.

Reb Saunders also struggles with the concept of choice. He chooses to raise Danny in silence, even though he understands that doing so in America will probably drive Danny away from his Hasidic roots. Nevertheless, Reb Saunders believes it is more important for Danny to cultivate his soul than for him to continue the family legacy. At the same time, the method Reb Saunders chooses for Danny is the one that was also chosen for him. Reb Saunders only knows the tradition in which he was raised. He has chosen to raise Danny to be a fuller human being, but does not know how to do so without forgoing a fuller, closer relationship with his son.

Throughout the book, all the characters struggle with the tension between accepting what has been chosen and choosing one's own path. Both options have advantages and disadvantages, privileges and obligations. Potok does not imply that actively making a choice is better than passively accepting what has been chosen. Rather, he stresses the value of both active engagement and passive reception.

MOTIFS

Motifs are recurring structures, contrasts, or literary devices that can help to develop and inform the text's major themes.

FATHER-SON RELATIONSHIPS

The epigraph of Book One of *The Chosen* is a quotation from Proverbs that highlights the importance of father-son relationships in the novel: "I was a son to my father. . . . And he taught me and said to me, 'Let your heart hold fast my words. . . .'" Because it is from the Bible, this quotation also points to the connection between obedience to one's father and obedience to God and religion. The critic Edward Abramson explains that *The Chosen*'s "stress upon fathers parallels a similar stress in Judaism, where God is King, Judge, and Father. . . . [T]he father can be viewed as a fount of wisdom, one who takes upon himself some of the aura of the Godhead." David

MOTIFS

Malter and Reb Saunders both possess profound knowledge and deep spiritual commitment, qualities they pass on to their sons. Yet, the two fathers interpret Judaism in contrasting ways. In particular, they have different beliefs about what their commitments to the outside world should be. These differences in beliefs inform how each father teaches and relates to his son, and how each son develops and matures.

As both Reb Saunders and David Malter emphasize, we are able to choose our friends, but not our fathers. This difference between friendships and father-son relationships adds another shade of meaning to the novel's title: fathers and sons cannot choose each other, but this lack of choice does not make their relationships any less meaningful. By the end of the book, all the characters have learned that one must strike a balance between what one can choose and what has been chosen for one. Danny chooses his own path, but he has also learned the value of being a tzaddik and the value of his family's heritage. Potok's message is that although we do not choose our fathers and sons, we must appreciate and respect them.

PERCEPTION

Ten of *The Chosen*'s eighteen chapters conclude with references to eyes, seeing, watching, looking, or listening. Perception and vision is the novel's dominant motif, bridging the entire text from Reuven's eye injury at the beginning to the final passage, in which Reuven watches Danny walk away after perceiving an "almost blinding" "light" in Danny's eyes. Vision in the novel symbolizes the ability to see the world, to see oneself, and to see beneath the surface and into the heart of a matter. As Danny and Reuven mature over the course of the novel, they develop clearer pictures of themselves and of the world around them.

After Reuven's eye accident, he remarks that "everything looks different." His experience in the hospital gives him a newfound appreciation of his own health. Later, his friendship with Danny teaches him to look beyond superficial appearances. Their friendship broadens and deepens Reuven's perception of the world and allows him to relate to and empathize with others' suffering.

As the novel progresses, Potok focuses on other senses besides vision. In Chapter 7, Reb Saunders scolds Danny for hearing but not listening. When Danny reads in the library, he covers his ears to block out sound. As Danny's friendship with Reuven develops, he learns to be a better listener. As a result of Danny's experience with silence—which parallels Reuven's experience with blindness—Danny learns to appreciate words. Furthermore, Reuven's development is apparent in his descriptive language, which becomes more specific throughout the novel. As he becomes more aware of the world around him, his descriptions become more detailed, displaying Reuven's improved command of his senses. The novel's final passage mentions four of the five senses, showing the development both Reuven and Danny have experienced over the course of the novel.

SUFFERING

The characters in *The Chosen* experience some suffering: Reuven is hospitalized after being hit by a baseball, Danny struggles with his father, and David Malter suffers two heart attacks. For the most part, however, the characters lead calm, happy, fulfilling lives, while the world suffers in the background of the novel. For instance, in the hospital, Mr. Savo, Billy Merrit, and Mickey all suffer far more than Reuven does. David Malter's heart attacks are overshadowed by the news of FDR's death and by the terrible revelations of the Holocaust.

Over the course of the novel, Reuven and Danny develop and mature as they learn important truths about the world around them and about themselves. Throughout this journey, they become increasingly aware of and sympathetic to the suffering around them. This increased awareness then leads to empathy, humility, and a sense of responsibility—all of which make both Reuven and Danny better people. David Malter and Reb Saunders both display a deep awareness of suffering, and both stress to their sons the importance of empathy. Even though David Malter criticizes Reb Saunders's zealousness and radical methods, he and Reb Saunders both want to teach Reuven and Danny to cultivate their souls and to care for others. Reb Saunders explains that our knowledge of the suffering of others erases our selfishness and makes us more empathetic and humble. It makes us aware of how frail and tiny we are and of how much we must depend upon the "Master of the Universe."

SYMBOLS

Symbols are objects, characters, figures, or colors used to represent abstract ideas or concepts.

EYES AND EYEGLASSES

The prevalence of eyes and eyeglasses in *The Chosen* reflects the novel's emphasis on perception of the world and of oneself. Eyes and eyeglasses represent vision, not only in the literal sense, but also in a broader, figurative sense. After injuring his eye, Reuven develops a better appreciation of his eyesight. At the beginning of Danny and Reuven's friendship, Danny works to make Reuven more aware and more willing to open his eyes to the world. As Danny develops an increased awareness of the world beyond his Hasidic community, his eyes grow weary and he begins to wear glasses.

Eyes are not just used for looking; they are also meant to be looked at. The way characters' eyes reveal their interior states implies that perception is a two-way process, not only about looking but about studying and receiving as well. When angry and withdrawn, David Malter's eyes become dark. When pleased and proud, Reb Saunders's eyes mist over. David Malter uses the eye as an example of the miracle of life, saying, "the eye that blinks, that is something." Mentions of eyes in the novel symbolize the importance of perception, and also the way reciprocity can improve perception.

THE TALMUD

Throughout *The Chosen*, there is only limited discussion of the Torah, the Jewish Bible and most holy of texts, and almost no mention of the Kabbalah, the mystic literature that is very important to Hasidic tradition. Instead, Potok places an unusual emphasis on the Talmud, which contains a series of commentaries by rabbis. Study of the Talmud, as demonstrated in the novel, involves active engagement of its commentaries and a willingness to challenge the text and to resolve conflicting points. Therefore, Potok's emphasis on Talmudic study in *The Chosen* symbolizes the importance of actively engaging tradition and pursuing knowledge in order to attain a unique and personal interpretation of Judaism and the world in general.

SUMMARY & ANALYSIS

CHAPTER I

SUMMARY: CHAPTER I

I stood in that room for a long time, watching the
sunlight and listening to the sounds on the street
outside. I stood there, tasting the room and the sunlight
and the sounds, and thinking of the long hospital ward.
(See QUOTATIONS, *p. 65)*

The narrator, Reuven Malter, describes the neighborhood in Williamsburg, Brooklyn, where he has lived for the first fifteen years of his life. Reuven's neighborhood is populated by Orthodox Jews, including some Hasidic sects. All the children attend yeshivas—Jewish parochial schools—in the area. Reuven then mentions Danny Saunders, a Hasidic friend. Danny and Reuven grew up five blocks away from each other. However, Reuven explains, the two never met because Danny's Hasidic community kept to itself, remaining fiercely loyal to its own synagogue and customs. Reuven notes that he probably would never have met Danny if not for the competitive Jewish sports leagues created during World War II.

One June afternoon, Reuven's Orthodox Jewish high school softball team plays a game against Danny's Hasidic team. As Reuven's team warms up, his enthusiastic and martial coach, Mr. Galanter, shouts out instructions and encouragements. Meanwhile, Reuven's friend, Davey Cantor, warns Reuven that their opponents, students at a very religious yeshiva, are "murderers." When the yeshiva boys arrive dressed in their traditional religious garb, Reuven doubts that they will pose a serious challenge.

The rabbi accompanying the yeshiva team insists that his boys practice for five minutes on the field before the game begins, and Mr. Galanter reluctantly agrees. Reuven notices one particularly strong batter on the yeshiva team, whom Davey identifies as Danny Saunders, the son of Reb Saunders.

Just before the game begins, the rabbi and coach of Danny's team tells his boys to "remember why and for whom we play." The Hasidic team bats first, and Reuven takes his position at second base. After the first two hitters are retired, the third, a bullish boy named Dov Shlomowitz, smacks a line drive. On his way around the base path, Dov charges into Reuven, knocking him down. Danny Saunders bats next, and hits the ball directly at the pitcher's head, forcing the pitcher to dive off the mound. Danny makes it safely to second base, and between batters, Reuven congratulates Danny on his hit. Danny identifies Reuven as the son of David Malter, who writes articles on the Talmud. He tells Reuven, "We're going to kill you apikorsim this afternoon." Reuven, struck by Danny's rudeness, sarcastically tells him to rub his tzitzit—traditional fringe—for good luck.

The next time Danny is up at bat, he again smacks the ball over the pitcher's head, but Reuven makes a remarkable leaping catch. By the top half of the fifth and final inning, Reuven's team is leading five to three. Reuven takes over as pitcher and baffles the first hitter he faces, Dov Shlomowitz, with his wicked curveball. Danny bats next and rings up two strikes as Reuven's curve dives below Danny's swing. Reuven then pitches two balls, but by Reuven's fifth pitch, Danny adjusts to the diving action of the curve. He deliberately swings low and crushes a line drive back toward the mound. Reuven brings his glove to his face to catch the ball, but it hits the tip of his glove and bounces back onto his glasses, shattering them. While lying on the ground, Reuven imagines he sees Danny smiling at the injury. Reuven sits out for the rest of the game and watches his team lose eight to seven. After the game, Mr. Galanter calls a cab to take him to the hospital.

ANALYSIS: CHAPTER 1

Potok focuses on a handful of motifs and themes in *The Chosen*, carefully weaving them throughout the entire novel. The world of the novel is a carefully controlled, patiently manipulative, and exclusive environment, much like the Jewish communities of Williamsburg in which Danny and Reuven grow up. Both the novel and Williamsburg communities operate as self-contained environments, within which Potok carefully selects and highlights particular details.

All of the novel's themes, which develop as the novel progresses, are introduced in this first chapter. The first of these themes involves complementary and contrasting pairs of characters and ideas. *The Chosen* is constructed around a seemingly endless series of these pairs, the most obvious of which is Reuven and Danny. While the two boys' individual situations contrast with one another, the boys also parallel each other in many ways. Each is the star of his softball team, and each makes an intelligent adjustment within the game—Reuven to catch Danny's line drive, Danny to hit Reuven's curveball—that proves crucial to the game's outcome. The most obvious trait shared by Reuven and Danny is their Judaism. Both boys are clearly devoted to their religion, and they wear clothing that marks them as observant Jews in the eyes of mainstream American society.

However, Danny, who is Hasidic, is part of a very different sect of Judaism than Reuven, who is Orthodox. Danny's earlocks and beard differentiate him from Reuven, who is clean-shaven. As the game progresses, Reuven and Danny come into conflict about their differing beliefs, to the point where the game itself becomes a kind of holy war. The warlike game parallels World War II, during which the novel is set. This parallel introduces the boys' relationship to the larger world around them, another important connection in the book. Mr. Galanter's constant use of military metaphors makes this relationship between the game and the war explicit, as does the boys' own perception that the game has become a battle of epic proportions.

At the same time, many facets of the game highlight its difference and separation from mainstream American life. It is a softball game, not a baseball game, played on blacktop, not on grass. Overall, the image of skullcapped youths playing baseball is unusual and strange. Throughout the book, the characters struggle to figure out how to reconcile their Jewish faith and tradition with modern American society. In general, the novel isolates its characters, so that all the characters, though they may come into conflict with one another, seem isolated as a group from mainstream American life.

The characters' isolation relates to the idea that Jews are "the chosen people," a community set apart from the rest of the world. Despite Danny and Reuven's religious differences, each must deal with the fact that, by virtue of his birth, he belongs to the Jewish tradition. As Jews, both Reuven and Danny must deal with religious commitments and responsibilities that most children their age do not have to encounter. The image of the all-Jewish softball game, foreign to most American readers, highlights the fact that both boys share a culture that is struggling to find its place in America.

Finally, this chapter introduces the motifs of vision and suffering. Acts of seeing, watching, perceiving, and reading are important in novel. When Reuven is hit in the eye with a ball, his vision and his perception of the world are placed in serious jeopardy. Significantly, Danny's relationship with Reuven begins as a result of pain that Danny inflicts upon Reuven. Suffering is a general motif in Jewish tradition and literature, and its full significance within *The Chosen* becomes more apparent as the novel progresses.

CHAPTER 2

SUMMARY: CHAPTER 2

Mr. Galanter and Reuven arrive at Brooklyn Memorial Hospital. A young doctor examines Reuven, who is feeling increasingly nauseous and dizzy. After the doctor realizes that Reuven was wearing glasses when he was hit, he calls in two more doctors to look at his eye, including Dr. Snydman, a warm and sympathetic eye expert. After examining Reuven, Dr. Snydman sends him upstairs to the eye ward. In the elevator on the way to the ward, Reuven sees flashing lights and swirling colors, and soon he is unconscious.

Reuven awakes to find himself in the hospital's sunlit eye ward. His bed lies between the beds of two other patients. To his left is a friendly man in his mid-thirties named Tony Savo. Tony, a professional prizefighter, speaks using boxing metaphors, referring to Reuven's head as "the old punching bag" and to his injury as a "clop." To Reuven's right is Billy, a spirited and optimistic blind boy aged ten or eleven. Billy explains that he lost his sight in a car accident, but will soon undergo an operation that will allow him to see again. Reuven tells Tony and Billy to call him Bobby, since his English name is Robert Malter. While they are talking, a nurse named Mrs. Carpenter brings dinner, assuring Reuven that all the food is kosher.

David Malter, Reuven's father, visits and informs Reuven that Dr. Snydman has operated on his eye. He assures Reuven that everything is all right, but Reuven realizes that his father is not being completely truthful. Finally, Mr. Malter reluctantly admits that the doctor is worried that, in the process of healing, scar tissue may grow over the pupil, blinding Reuven's left eye. He also tells Reuven that Reb Saunders has been calling him to ask about Reuven's condition. Reuven grows angry and argues that Danny intentionally hit him. He also tells his father that Danny called him an apikorsim. David Malter is shocked by Reuven's accusations and remains critical of them.

Mr. Malter informs Reuven that he cannot read at all until his eye has healed. He gives Reuven a portable radio, instructing him to remain aware of news of the War. He also brings Reuven his tefillin and prayer book. Throughout the conversation, David Malter looks sickly. Reuven, upset to see his father looking so tired and unkempt, reminds his father to take care of his own health. David Malter leaves, and Reuven falls asleep thinking about Billy, wondering what it is like to be blind.

ANALYSIS: CHAPTER 2

Reuven's traumatic eye injury underscores the importance and fragility of the eyes, an important means of connection to the world around us. In his closing words of Chapter 2, Reuven says he can't imagine what it would be like to be blind and not notice any difference when opening his eyes, to find "everything ... still dark." Reuven's comment alludes to the beginning of Genesis, the first book of the Old Testament: "In the beginning when God created the heavens and the earth, the earth was a formless void and darkness covered the face of the deep. . . . Then God said, 'Let there be light'; and there was light. And God saw that the light was good; and God separated the light from the darkness" (Gen. 1:1–4). The Bible equates darkness with hopelessness, with a world without God. For Reuven, blindness would also be hopeless because he loves to read, and because reading is an important part of both prayer and learning. Reuven fears that without his eyesight, he will be closed off from the world of ideas, the world of his friends and family, and the world of God.

At the same time, the fragility of Reuven's vision and of the healing process implies that one's way of seeing the world can be altered. Reuven's eye injury foreshadows the coming radical change to his opinion of Danny. Just as Reuven's eye heals and he learns to see again, so too does he eventually learn to see Danny—and the whole world—differently. In this chapter, vision operates on two levels. It is a physical ability that enables learning, prayer, and interaction with others, but it also represents the more abstract act of seeing and judging others. Both these aspects of vision are connected to one another, and both are important to understanding the novel.

When Reuven's father visits, we see that his and Reuven's relationship is one of love, respect, and mutual concern. They worry about each other's health and discuss their feeling with ease, and they share a strong devotion to religion. For example, David brings tefillin and prayer books to the hospital, so his son can stay devoted to his faith. At the same time, David Malter stresses Reuven's obli-

SUMMARY & ANALYSIS

gation to care about the outside world as strongly as he cares about religion by bringing Reuven a radio and telling him that being hospitalized shouldn't mean being shut off from the world.

CHAPTER 3

SUMMARY: CHAPTER 3

Reuven awakes to commotion in the hospital and the sound of the radio. Mr. Savo tells him that it is D-Day: the Allied forces have landed on the coast of France. For the rest of the morning, Mr. Savo, Billy, and Reuven excitedly listen to news of the war. As he listens to his radio, Reuven prays fervently with his tefillin. Mr. Savo asks why he is so religious, and Reuven reveals that he plans to become a rabbi.

After lunch, a sickly six-year-old patient walks into the ward and asks to play catch with Mr. Savo. Mr. Savo explains that the boy, named Mickey, has been hospitalized for most of his life due to a strange stomach condition. Thinking about such a tragic situation, Mr. Savo tells Reuven that they live in a "[c]razy world. Cockeyed." Savo plays catch with Mickey, but the nurse scolds him. Mr. Savo's condition is apparently much worse than he has let on, and the exertion of playing catch pains him.

Soon after, Mr. Galanter comes to pay Reuven a brief visit. He and Reuven discuss the invasion, and Reuven mentions that Billy's uncle is a bomber pilot. Billy eagerly joins the conversation, asking Mr. Galanter why he is not fighting in the war, assuming that he was injured overseas. Mr. Galanter becomes extremely embarrassed, and hints at a physical condition that prevents him from serving. Reuven feels bad for his teacher's embarrassment and, after Mr. Galanter leaves, Reuven falls asleep thinking about him, while continuing to fear for his own eye.

Reuven is awakened by a figure standing by his bed. When he opens his good eye, he is shocked to see Danny Saunders. Danny tries to apologize for injuring Reuven, but Reuven rudely dismisses him. Immediately, Reuven feels foolish for having treated Danny in such a way. Later that evening, Reuven's father comes to visit. After he hears about the encounter with Danny, he reprimands Reuven. After Mr. Malter leaves, Roger Merrit, Billy's father, introduces himself to Reuven. He asks Reuven to call Billy at home after he leaves the hospital, and Reuven agrees.

The next day, Danny returns and Reuven apologizes for his rudeness. Danny sits down at the edge of Reuven's bed and tells him that he had wanted to kill him during the ball game, but he cannot understand why. When Reuven compliments Danny on his playing, Danny tells Reuven that his father permits him to practice baseball and read books only after he completes his required daily quota of Talmud—an astounding four pages a day. Danny reveals that this burden is in fact quite easy for him, because he has a photographic memory. He further explains that he is expected to take his father's place as rabbi and leader of their Hasidic community, even though he would rather become a psychologist. Reuven, in turn, says that his father would like him to become a mathematician, but he is more interested in becoming a rabbi. Danny also reveals a curious fact about his father. Reb Saunders believes that "words distort what a person really feels in his heart," and he "wishes everyone could talk in silence." Danny leaves, promising to return the next day.

ANALYSIS: CHAPTER 3

Chapter 3 begins with a lengthy description of the patients' reaction to D-day, highlighting the historical circumstances of the novel's setting. At first glance, this may appear to be a digression that has little or nothing to do with the main story about the relationship between Danny and Reuven. However, world events—and the characters' reactions and relations to these events—play an important role in *The Chosen*. The events of World War II are important to Jewish history as well as to world history in general, and in later chapters, we see that Danny and Reuven's relationship is inseparable from its historical context. Specifically, the Holocaust and its ramifications for the global Jewish community force the characters to examine the relationship between tradition and modernity.

Despite the differences between Reuven's and Danny's beliefs, both boys exist in Jewish communities that are markedly different from mainstream American culture. Furthermore, as Danny and Reuven talk in earnest for the first time, their similarities surprise them. Reuven is surprised by Danny's perfect English speech and openness about his feelings—Danny does not fit Reuven's stereotypes about Hasids. Reuven is learning to see Danny differently, by looking beyond superficial appearances. Reuven finds he and Danny have a lot in common, including an intense competitive drive and a fervent intellectual passion.

SUMMARY & ANALYSIS

The parallel-but-opposite nature of Reuven's and Danny's situations emphasizes the difference in their relationships with their respective fathers. Danny wants to become an intellectual, but feels obligated to become a rabbi; whereas Reuven wants to become a rabbi, but feels pressure from his father to be an intellectual. Although Reuven does not discuss his own upbringing in this chapter, we see in Chapter 2 that Reuven and David Malter have an open, easy relationship built upon mutual concern and respect. In Chapter 3, Danny's descriptions of Reb Saunders's dominating parenting—the intense daily Talmud study he prescribes, his strong feelings against the apikorsim, his refusal to write or speak to his son—set up a contrast between Reb Saunders and David Malter, and between the two father-son relationships in the book. The contrasts between Danny and Reuven primarily revolve around the issue of choice. Danny is surprised that Reuven has chosen to become a rabbi, and then resignedly describes his own situation by emphasizing that he has no choice but to take father's place.

CHAPTER 4

SUMMARY: CHAPTER 4

David Malter visits Reuven again and tells him Dr. Snydman will examine his eye on Friday morning. Afterward, Reuven probably will be able to come home. Reuven tells his father about Danny's last visit and comments that the way Danny looks does not match the way he speaks. Danny dresses like a Hasid, he says, but talks about *Ivanhoe* and Freud. Reuven's father encourages him to befriend Danny, citing a Talmudic maxim that stresses the importance of choosing a friend for oneself. He also says, "A Greek philosopher said that two people who are true friends are like two bodies with one soul." After Mr. Malter leaves, Mr. Savo warns Reuven to beware of fanatics like Danny. Reuven wakes up in the middle of the night and is concerned to see a curtain around Mr. Savo's bed. The curtain is still up the next morning, and Reuven hears bustling activity and soft moaning from Mr. Savo's bed. In the early evening, Danny comes to visit for a third time. Reuven is excited by Danny's visit but worried about Mr. Savo, so he suggests they go into the hall to talk.

Reuven and Danny have a long conversation about their intellectual interests and their aspirations for the future. They discover that they were both born in the same place, Brooklyn Memorial Hospital, where Reuven is currently staying. Danny elaborates on his father's belief in silence, saying that his father never speaks to him except when they are studying Torah and Talmud. Danny also confesses that even though his father tells him man's mission in life is to obey God, sometimes he is not sure what God wants. Danny knows that he is expected to take his father's place as head of the Hasidic dynasty, but he is not sure he wants to do so.

Reuven is surprised by Danny's confession and even more shocked when Danny reveals that he reads seven or eight non-religious books a week, including writings by authors like the evolutionists Darwin and T. H. Huxley, of whom Reb Saunders would not approve. Danny tells Reuven that a nice man in the library recommends books for him to read. Reuven tells Danny he doesn't know what to make of him, saying, "You look like a Hasid, but you don't sound like one."

After a silence, Reuven tells Danny about his love for mathematics. Danny knows little about math, and he is excited that Reuven knows so much about a subject he knows nothing about. In the middle of their conversation, Reuven's father comes to visit, and both boys are astonished to learn that Mr. Malter is the man who has been recommending books to Danny in the library. Reuven is stunned and a little hurt that his father said nothing to him about this activity, but David Malter explains that he was only trying to respect Danny's privacy. After recovering from his initial shock, Danny thanks Mr. Malter for all his reading recommendations and promises to visit Reuven on Saturday afternoon, after he is home from the hospital.

When Reuven wakes up on Friday morning, the curtain is no longer drawn around Mr. Savo's bed, but Billy's bed is now empty. Mr. Savo tells Reuven that Billy is undergoing the operation to restore his sight. Reuven prays for Billy and then nervously goes to have his examination with Dr. Snydman. The doctor examines Reuven and tells him that he thinks the scar tissue will heal correctly. Reuven is very excited to return home, and he says goodbye to Mr. Savo. Before he leaves, he learns that Mr. Savo's bad eye had to be removed.

ANALYSIS: CHAPTER 4

Like Chapter 3, Chapter 4 contains many scenes that do not directly relate to the novel's main story about the relationship between Reuven and Danny. Potok details Reuven's reaction to Mr. Savo's surgery, and he emphasizes Billy Merrit's surgery. The chapter ends with the news that Mr. Savo has to have his eye removed, a revelation that reminds Reuven and us of the presence of suffering, especially undeserved or needless suffering. We pity Mr. Savo and Billy because their injuries are horrible and arose through no fault of their own. Potok intersperses examples of needless, random suffering throughout the novel to reinforce suffering as a fundamental, ever-present aspect of human existence.

Over the course of Reuven and Danny's long conversation, we see that the two boys have much in common. They share a ravenous intellectual curiosity, they both study Talmud diligently, they both evidence a deep commitment to and respect for Jewish tradition, they are both taught by David Malter, and they were even born in the same hospital. More important, we see how they complement each other: Danny is interested in science and the humanities, while Reuven's strength is in mathematics. Danny is delighted to learn that Reuven knows so much about a subject with which he is unfamiliar because he sees that Reuven is an intellectual equal who can teach him about things he cannot learn on his own. Throughout *The Chosen*, all the characters hunger for knowledge, and Danny's excitement over Reuven's ability to teach him foreshadows the mutually beneficial role the boys will play in each other's life. Each will teach and be taught by the other.

The epigraph of Book One of *The Chosen* is a quotation from Proverbs. It reads, "I was a son to my father. . . . And he taught me and said to me, 'Let your heart hold fast my words. . . .'" This quotation emphasizes the importance of teaching imparted by a father to a son, and it is in his relationship to his father that Reuven's situation differs most strikingly from Danny's. Whereas Reuven's father speaks to Reuven freely about all subjects, Reb Saunders only teaches Danny about Jewish law and custom. Reb Saunders attempts to restrict his son's education to Hasidic customs and precepts, reflecting a small-minded and limited worldview in which such topics are the only ones worth learning.

Reb Saunders's silence seems unusually cruel and inexplicable, and his lack of non-liturgical interaction seems to imply a fundamental distance or coldness in his relationship with Danny. But in this chapter, Potok hints that silence doesn't always imply coldness and distance when, after Danny reveals his doubts about God's will and Reuven responds, the two boys "[sit] in silence a long time. It was a warm silence, though, not in the least bit awkward." This brief passage foreshadows the multifaceted role silence plays later in the novel.

When Reuven says to Danny, "You look like a Hasid, but you don't sound like one," he shows that one's senses can contradict and complement one another, each offering insight into the world that the others lack. Although Reuven's eye heals completely, his experience in the hospital teaches him how fragile his vision is, both literally (in terms of the injury to his eye) and figuratively (in terms of his misperceptions about Danny). By listening to Danny, Reuven learns aspects of his friend that his eyes could never see.

CHAPTERS 5–6

SUMMARY: CHAPTER 5

Reuven and his father take a cab home from the hospital back to their brownstone apartment on a street off of Lee Avenue. When Reuven enters the house, he can smell the delicious chicken soup that Manya, their Russian housekeeper, has prepared for them. Manya greets Reuven warmly.

After lunch, Reuven walks through his apartment as if seeing it for the first time. First, he walks through the hallway, which is lined with pictures of great Zionists from the past century: Theodor Herzl, the founder of modern Zionism; Chaim Nachman Bialik, a great Hebrew poet and writer; and Chaim Weizmann, a Zionist leader who eventually becomes the first president of Israel. Next, Reuven surveys his own room, where New York Times war maps line the wall alongside pictures of Roosevelt and Einstein. He then enters his father's study, which is lined from floor to ceiling with bookcases.

Reuven's father is working at his typewriter so Reuven exits quickly, not wanting to disturb him. In the living room, Reuven looks through the window, watching the sunlight. He remembers that Danny has promised to visit him the following day. Lying on the lounge chair on the back porch, Reuven thinks about Danny and about all that has changed since the softball game.

SUMMARY: CHAPTER 6

That night, after Shabbat dinner, Reuven sits at the kitchen table with his father, who sips tea and answers Reuven's questions about Danny. Mr. Malter warns Reuven that he will begin his explanation far back in history, with a description of the rise of Hasidism in the eighteenth century. In the seventeenth century, David Malter explains, Polish Jews were persecuted by Polish peasants and by members of the Greek Orthodox Church. As a result of the anti-Semitism, someone pretending to be a messiah deceived them. Serious Jewish faith in Poland was replaced by a superficial belief in magic and superstition. A leader named the Ba'al Shem Tov—The Kind or Good Master of the Name—emerged into this spiritual void with a new vision of Judaism, and Hasidism was born.

Ba'al Shem Tov studied the Jewish mystical texts of the Kabbalah, and downplayed the study of Jewish legal texts in favor of spirituality and prayer. Every Hasidic community was led by a tzaddik, a righteous person who served as a superhuman link between the community and God. The Hasidim lived shut off from the rest of the world and passed down the position of tzaddik from father to son. Despite opposition from the Mitnagdim—the intellectual opponents of Hasidism—the movement flourished, and its traditions were passed down through the generations. David Malter points out that the clothes the Hasidim wear today are the same style they wore in Poland hundreds of years ago, and that they hold many unique beliefs, such as the belief that Hasidic leaders need to bear the suffering of the entire Jewish People. Reuven's explains that Danny is next in line to inherit his father's great Hasidic dynasty, with all its traditions and customs.

Mr. Malter says that because Danny is so brilliant, he is not satisfied with Jewish texts alone but voraciously consumes all types of literature. In fact, Danny reminds Mr. Malter of Solomon Maimon, an eighteenth-century Jew who forsook his faith to pursue secular knowledge. Mr. Malter encourages Reuven to become friends with Danny, then apologizes for his long lecture. Reuven tells his father how different the world looks to him now, as a result of only the last five days. Reuven gets up to go to bed, leaving his father to sip his tea pensively at the kitchen table.

ANALYSIS: CHAPTERS 5–6

Potok unconventionally waits until the middle of the novel to provide us with descriptions of the world of the characters. Up to this point, *The Chosen* has consisted primarily of conversations, with brief interludes for Reuven's reflections. It therefore seems strange that Reuven gives us a long, detailed account of his apartment, a place he has lived his entire life. But Reuven's description emphasizes the way his time in the hospital has changed his way of under-standing the world as well as his opinion of Danny. Upon his return, Reuven remarks that the hydrangea bush, something he had never really noticed, "seemed suddenly luminous and alive." Later, he comments that after his five days in the hospital, "the world around seemed sharpened now and pulsing with life." Reuven's encounter with suffering has taught him to appreciate his own life more and has sharpened his perception of the world as a result.

Reuven's description of his apartment reveals the Malter house-hold's dual emphasis on religion and modern intellectualism. Jewish culture runs strong through the house, from the food Reuven eats for lunch to the portraits of Zionists that hang on the wall. Yet there is an even stronger emphasis on intellectualism and current events, as shown in the war maps on the wall, the picture of Albert Einstein, and David Malter's massive, book-lined study. All of these items illustrate a love of learning and a commitment to connecting to the world that lies beyond the boundaries of strict Jewish tradition.

David Malter's lecture in Chapter 6 reinforces his commitment to intellectual engagement. Throughout his lengthy speech, Reuven's father displays patience, love, respect, and concern for his son, apologizing for droning on and making sure that Reuven fol-lows his explanations. As Mr. Malter speaks, he reveals his breadth of knowledge as well as Reuven's enthusiasm for learning. Indi-rectly, Mr. Malter's lesson to Reuven underscores the power and importance of communication between father and son, an aspect lacking in Danny's relationship with his father.

In general, David Malter's explanation of Hasidism is important to our understanding of Danny's relationship with his father. Mr. Malter's comment about the difficulties of being a tzaddik, or buffer, in a community foreshadows the consequences of Reuven's future involvement with Danny and Reb Saunders. David Malter's speech demonstrates that no single, monolithic Jewish tradition exists. Rather, many different systems of belief are subsumed under the cat-egory of "Jewish." These differing groups often are bitterly opposed to one another, particularly when it comes to the issues of Jewish heritage, history, and belief.

CHAPTER 7

SUMMARY: CHAPTER 7

"We are commanded to study His Torah! We are commanded to sit in the light of the Presence! It is for this that we were created!"

(See QUOTATIONS, *p. 67)*

Reuven and his father wake up early on Shabbat morning and walk to synagogue together. They return home, eat lunch, and then Reuven falls asleep thinking about the colors of Billy's and Danny's eyes.

Three hours later, Reuven wakes to find Danny standing over him. Danny suggests they walk over to his shul so that Reuven can meet Reb Saunders. As they walk, the boys tell each other about their families. Reuven explains he has no siblings because his mother died shortly after he was born. Danny says he has a younger sister and a younger brother. The boys then discover that they were born only two days apart. Danny also explains that his father is a great man who saved the members of his community from persecution by bringing them to America after World War I, a journey made in the face of great adversity. He also explains that Reb Saunders' older brother vanished, so Reb Saunders inherited his father's position. Danny notes that because his father is a tzaddik, considered a bridge between his followers and God, his congregation will follow him anywhere.

At Danny's father's shul, Reuven and Danny meet a crowd of black-caftaned Hasids who part like the Red Sea when Danny approaches. As the boys enter the brownstone, Danny explains that the shul is on the bottom floor and his family lives on the top two stories.

The synagogue soon fills with Hasidim who have come for the afternoon service. Two men approach Danny and ask him to resolve an argument over a passage of Talmud, which Danny interprets masterfully. Danny's father comes downstairs, and the room is suddenly quiet. Danny introduces his friend to his father, and Reb Saunders remarks that he is interested in getting to know the son of David Malter.

Following the afternoon service, the men sit down at the table for a ritual Shabbat meal led by Reb Saunders. He concludes the meal with an impassioned talk, using Talmudic quotes from several great rabbis to argue that Jews are obligated to serve God's will by studying Torah. It is through the study of Torah, Reb Saunders says, that God listens to mankind. Reb Saunders also uses gematriya—numerological manipulations of Hebrew words and phrases—to prove his point.

Following his talk, Reb Saunders asks Danny if he noticed any mistakes or inconsistencies in his argument. Danny replies that his father misattributed one quote. Reb Saunders then asks Danny several detailed follow-up questions, and the two launch into an extended discussion of Talmudic precepts. The assembled crowd of Hasidim is obviously pleased by Danny's quick and sharp answers. Reuven realizes that the whole speech was one great quiz—Reb Saunders made deliberate errors to see if his son would notice and correct him.

Finally, Reb Saunders asks Danny if there were any additional mistakes. When Danny shakes his head, Reb Saunders quietly chastises him for not listening carefully and turns to Reuven, asking the same question. Reuven, terrified and astonished that he is being asked to correct a great tzaddik, tentatively points out a mistake in Reb Saunders's gematriya. Reb Saunders and Danny, along with the entire crowd, are delighted at Reuven's intelligence.

After the evening service, Reb Saunders praises Reuven and approves of his friendship with Danny. Danny walks Reuven part of the way home, and the boys happily discover that they both plan to study at the same Jewish college following high school.

Reuven returns home and finds that his father has been worried about him because he has been out so late. Reuven apologizes and tells his father about his experience at Reb Saunders's shul, noting that he thought Reb Saunders's quiz was cruel. David Malter replies that it is important to display knowledge in public, but that he finds Reb Saunders's intentional mistakes distasteful. Mr. Malter then says he is proud of his son. He reminds Reuven not to read until his eye heals, and then they go to sleep.

ANALYSIS: CHAPTER 7

Chapter 7 is a crucial turning point in *The Chosen*, marking Reuven's entry into Danny Saunders's world. Potok begins the chapter by focusing upon Reuven's Shabbat experience with his own father, allowing us to contrast David Malter's religious worship with Reb Saunders's. At first, this contrast seems stark and obvious. Reb Saunders is distant towards Danny, while David Malter is open and intimate with Reuven. Reb Saunders speaks furiously and almost demagogically about religion, while earlier in the chapter, we see David Malter praying silently and fervently. Reb Saunders preaches that the world is contaminated and implies that devout believers must remove themselves from all earthly concerns. In contrast, at the Malter's apartment, the litany of pictures and maps on the wall imply a commitment to and respect for earthly concerns.

However, upon closer inspection, there are many similarities between the two fathers. Both are devoutly committed to religion, and both share a deep, profound knowledge of Jewish law. Reuven is careful to point out that the Talmudic discussion between Danny and Reb Saunders isn't about showing off or impressing others with their brilliant arguments. Instead, Reuven says, "they seemed more interested in. . .straightforward knowledge." That David Malter supports Reb Saunder's public quizzes goes against our expectations and drives home the similarities between Reuven and Danny's fathers. David Malter's reaction to Reuven's story reminds us that Danny and Reuven's situations are not as different as they appear.

Several events in Chapter 7 enhance our understanding of other aspects of the novel. During Reb Saunder's quiz, Reuven sees Danny's face curl into the same vicious grin that Reuven saw at the softball game. Reuven is frightened, because he knows Danny makes this expression when he has the urge to kill someone. Danny's grimace recalls the anger and competitiveness of the softball game and connects his violent behavior at the game with his resentment toward his father. Another important revelation occurs when Reb Saunders mentions that the gematriya for chai, a significant Hebrew word meaning "life," is eighteen. We realize that *The Chosen* is divided into eighteen chapters in allusion to the numerical value of this important Hebrew word. Also, when Danny mentions that Reb Saunders became tzaddik because Reb Saunders's older brother abandoned the lineage, we see that Danny's own desire to abandon his traditional duty in order to study psychology is not new to his family. Danny's situation parallels the situation his uncle's a generation before.

At one point, Reb Saunders passionately declares, "It is not the world that is commanded to study Torah, but the people of Israel!" This statement underscores Reb Saunders's belief in a dichotomy between the outside world and Jewish tradition. On a deeper level,

Reb Saunders's statement refers to the novel's title, interpreting what it means to be a member of the "Chosen People." Reb Saunders argues that Jews, by virtue of their birth, must bear unique burdens that give privilege as well as obligation. This definition of "chosen" implies a sense of separation from the outside world, but also a sense of entitlement. Both Reuven and Danny struggle to reconcile their unique obligations with their feelings of obligation to the outside world.

CHAPTER 8

SUMMARY: CHAPTER 8

When Reuven returns to school, his friends treat him like a hero, but he feels they are acting immature. After school, he takes a trolley to the public library to meet Danny. He finds Danny on the third floor, where the scholarly journals and pamphlets are located. Reuven does not want to disturb Danny so he sits down at another table and reviews symbolic logic in his head. He is still not permitted to read because his eye has not healed completely.

Reuven joins Danny at his table so that he can hear him read aloud from Danny's book, Graetz's *History of the Jews*. Graetz's harsh denunciation of the Hasidim distresses Danny. Graetz argues that many tzaddiks, especially one whom Reb Saunders has taught Danny to revere, were con artists who took advantage of their followers. Reuven reminds Danny that he should not necessarily take Graetz's scholarship to heart. Danny then tells Reuven about the psychology text he has been reading concerning dreams and the unconscious.

Danny says he has been studying German so that he can read Freud, and Reuven is astonished, thinking about the parallels between Danny and Solomon Maimon. When Reuven tells his father about Danny's activities, David Malter marvels at Danny's curiosity and capacity for learning at such a young age. Later that week, Reuven's father confesses that he isn't sure whether it is ethical to give Danny books to read without his father's knowledge. At the same time, he recognizes that no one will stop Danny from reading and takes solace in the fact that, through frequent discussions, he will help Danny digest the material.

That Shabbat, Reuven goes over to Danny's brownstone, where he meets Danny's mother and beautiful sister. Danny and Reuven spend the afternoon studying Talmud with Reb Saunders on the third floor of the house, which bears a striking similarity to Reuven's own home. At first, the depth and intensity of the discussion between Reb Saunders astounds Reuven, but he soon realizes that, although Reuven lacks the breadth of Danny's knowledge, he is Danny's equal in depth.

Reb Saunders and Danny reach a stopping point in their discussion, and Reb Saunders sends his son to get some tea. In Danny's absence, Reb Saunders reveals to Reuven that he knows about his son's secret reading at the library and studying with Reuven's father. Reb Saunders asks Reuven to tell him what Danny has been reading, as he cannot ask his son directly. Reuven is unsure what to reveal, but he tells Reb Saunders everything except that Danny is learning German, wants to study Freud, and has read books on Hasidism. Later that evening, Danny walks Reuven home. Reuven confesses that he told Reb Saunders about Danny's library visits, and that Reb already knew about them. To Reuven's surprise, Danny is relieved that his father knows.

Danny explains that his father has raised him in silence. Ever since the age of ten or eleven, his father has talked to him only when they study Talmud together. Reb Saunders says that through silence, Danny will learn to look into his own soul for answers. Danny admits that he finds his father's methods of parenting perplexing, and Reuven agrees. Back at the Malter house, Reuven tells his father about Reb Saunders's silence. Although Mr. Malter seems to be familiar with that tradition, he refuses to explain it to Reuven. He does, however, say that Reb Saunders is using Reuven as a buffer through whom he can talk to Danny.

ANALYSIS: CHAPTER 8

Chapter 8 relates two separate study sessions: Danny and Reuven's secular session at the library and their Talmudic session in Reb Saunders's study. The beginning of the library session again underscores the way vision functions within the novel as a metaphor for seeing the world. Reuven is struck by the depiction of Homer's blindness in the mural in the library entrance. He is particularly sensitive to this portrayal because of his earlier eye injury, and he empathizes with Homer's handicap. Danny thinks that Reuven is asleep and rouses him in a scene that echoes Danny's first hospital visit to Reuven in Chapter 3. In that scene, Danny stood at Reuven's bedside and waited for him to wake up. Once again, Danny's presence forces Reuven to open his eyes and change his view of the world.

SUMMARY & ANALYSIS

At the library, Danny's perspective changes when he reads the depiction of Hasidism presented in Graetz's *History of the Jews*. That book, published in six volumes in 1846, was the first attempt to write the history of the Jews from a Jewish point of view. Graetz's contention that Judaism is a historical phenomenon that develops in time was rejected by his more Orthodox contemporaries, including Samson Raphael Hirsch, the namesake of the college that Reuven and Danny later attend.

Graetz's harsh words about Hasidism reinforce our sense of tensions within Judaism. Graetz argues that the Jews were formed by history and have developed throughout history. This perspective is problematic for more religious Jews, such as Reb Saunders, who see themselves as the inheritors of the religion of their God-chosen ancestors. This tension between an evolving Judaism and a static Judaism can be seen in the contrasting opinions of David Malter and Reb Saunders, as well as in the Zionist and anti-Zionist movements. Even more generally, such a tension is a part of any culture that struggles with a changing world and a desire to remain true to its history and traditions. Also notable at the library is the way Reuven finds Danny's life to uncannily parallel the life of Solomon Maimon, a young Polish Jew who lived in the second half of the eighteenth century. Solomon Maimon studied non-Jewish literature after the Talmud could not satisfy his hunger for knowledge, and as a result of his heresy, he died rootless and alone. Potok's inclusion of Maimon in the story provides suspense, as we hope Danny does not meet the same fate as his predecessor.

The geography of Reb Saunders's apartment replicates almost exactly the layout of the Malter's apartment, reinforcing the parallel nature of the two father-son relationships. Yet, where open communication exists between David Malter and Reuven, silence exists between Reb Saunders and Danny. Therefore, true to his father's prediction, Reuven finds himself in the uncomfortable role as a go-between for Danny and Reb Saunders. All parties involved are glad that Reuven and Reb Saunders's conversation takes place. Reb Saunders is curious to learn what books Danny is reading, Reuven feels compelled to educate Reb Saunders about his son's behavior in the library, and Danny is relieved to find out that his father knows about his library visits. The fact that breaking the silence makes everyone involved feel better implicitly undermines the value of Reb Saunders's practice of silence toward his son.

CHAPTERS 9–10

SUMMARY: CHAPTER 9

On Monday morning, Reuven's father takes him to Dr. Snydman's office for an eye examination. The doctor pronounces Reuven's eye perfectly healed and says he can read again. Reuven is excited to get back to his studies and to make up his exams.

That Friday, Reuven calls Roger Merrit, Billy's father, to ask him about Billy's eyesight. Mr. Merrit informs Reuven that Billy's surgery was unsuccessful. When Reuven asks if he can visit Billy, Mr. Merrit says his company has transferred him to Albany, and Billy has already moved there. When Reuven gets off the phone, his hands are freezing, and he cannot concentrate. He sits on his porch and watches a housefly trapped in a spider web. Reuven blows on the web to free the fly and watches as the spider tumbles from the broken web and disappears from view.

SUMMARY: CHAPTER 10

During the first month of summer, Reuven and Danny spend almost every day together. In the mornings, they study Talmud with their fathers—although Reuven spends three days a week playing ball instead of studying. In the afternoons, they read together in the public library. David Malter frequently joins them, quietly researching for an article he is writing. On Saturdays, Reuven and Danny discuss Talmud with Reb Saunders, but Danny's father does not ask Reuven any more questions about Danny's extracurricular activities. Danny and Reuven spend most evenings together, walking and talking, although occasionally Reuven goes to movies with his other friends, an activity from which Danny is prohibited. Reuven and his father devotedly follow the progress of the war in the newspapers, and Danny begins reading Freud in German.

One week, Reuven's father travels to Manhattan to do research. Reuven spends the week studying with Danny at the library. During this period, Danny is frustrated with Freud's German and seems stuck. Then one day, during a Talmud session with his father, Danny realizes that he must study Freud like he studies Talmud, with dictionaries and commentaries. Up to that point, Danny explains to Reuven, he had been reading Freud instead of studying him. He begins to make progress with this new approach.

Meanwhile, Reuven reads a book on symbolic logic. He lends Danny some books to read while Reuven and his father are at their cottage near Peekskill during the month of August. Upon Reuven's return, the boys meet in the library, and Danny is excited to discuss what he has learned about Freud. The two agree to talk about it in the near future, but as the new school year begins, Reuven becomes too busy to talk with Danny about Freud.

ANALYSIS: CHAPTERS 9–10

In Chapter 9, Reuven's conversation with Mr. Merritt about the failure of Billy's surgery forces Reuven to confront the existence of unjust suffering as he did in the hospital. He realizes that he has no control over such senseless pain. He also realizes that such pain is the result of nothing more than bad luck. In the face of such arbitrary cruelty, Reuven wonders how to make sense of the world around him, how to reconcile the idea of an all-powerful, all-knowing God with such random, senseless suffering. This conflict within Reuven foreshadows the struggle that the world's Jews—and the characters in the novel—face in the wake of the Holocaust.

At the end of Chapter 9, Potok abruptly changes the tone of the novel's narration, filling Reuven's description of the spider and housefly with symbolic language and imagery. The trapped fly symbolizes the cruelty and suffering that are an unavoidable part of the natural world. Reuven's freeing of the fly reflects his desire to alleviate this suffering. At the same time, in trying to help the fly, Reuven hurts the spider, which suggests that helping someone possibly and perhaps even necessarily hurts someone else.

Chapter 10 accelerates the story, relating the events of the entire summer in just a few pages. Previous chapters took place over the course of a day or two, and the duration of all of Book I (Chapters 1–4) is less than a week. Chapter 10's accelerated time frame, which continues for most of the remainder of the novel, reflects the accelerating maturity of both Danny and Reuven. They are growing up rapidly and acquiring more commitments and responsibilities. The frenetic pace introduced in Chapter 10 also reflects the increasingly frenetic pace of Reuven's and Danny's lives. At the end of the chapter, Reuven remarks, "for a long while I had no time at all to think about, let alone discuss, the writings of Sigmund Freud." To show that Reuven and Danny have less time for discussion and introspection, Potok relates fewer of Reuven's and Danny's thoughts and words.

SUMMARY & ANALYSIS

Chapter 10 also introduces a parallel between Danny's study of Freud and his study of the Talmud. By teaching Danny how to analyze Talmud, Reb Saunders unknowingly has equipped Danny with the skills he needs to understand Freud. Furthermore, Danny is using methods gleaned from his religious study to learn material that subverts his religious faith. This parallel makes us question whether Danny will be able to reconcile his conflicting obligations to his father and faith on the one hand, and his desires to pursue secular thought outside the bounds of his tradition on the other hand.

CHAPTERS 11–12

SUMMARY: CHAPTER 11

That school year, Reuven is elected president of his class. Although he and Danny still meet regularly on Shabbat afternoons, they never get around to discussing Freud. In the winter, the Germans launch a major offensive; everyone is preoccupied with the events of the war and with keeping track of American casualties. After several exciting rumors that the war is nearing an end, Danny catches the flu and is bedridden for a week.

On a Thursday afternoon in April, Reuven learns that President Roosevelt has passed away. The news devastates Reuven. He had thought of FDR as being immortal, and he compares hearing the news of his death to hearing that God died. He returns home to listen to the radio with his teary-eyed father. Less than a week after Roosevelt's death, Reuven comes home from school with a high fever and is bedridden for ten days. That May, Reb Saunders and Reuven's father also become sick. They are both seriously ill when the world learns that the War in Europe has ended.

At first everyone is joyous following the news of the surrender, but then the terrible reports of the German concentration camps shock and sadden the Jewish community. David Malter breaks down in tears, and Reuven is overwhelmed by the stories of destruction and devastation. Danny's father talks wistfully of the Jewish world in Europe and of the brutal persecution Jews have experienced throughout history. The next Shabbat, Danny and Reuven meet with Danny's father, but they do not study Talmud. Instead, Reb Saunders speaks mournfully about European Jewry and questions how God could let such terrible things happen. Reb Saunders's conclusion, that everything must be a part of God's will, is an answer neither Reuven nor his father can accept.

David Malter tells Reuven that it is up to Jews in America to preserve Jewish tradition, now that Hitler has destroyed most Jewish culture in Europe.

After Reuven's final exams that year, his father suffers a heart attack. In the first few frightening days following the episode, Reuven is cared for by Manya, the Malters' housekeeper, but soon Reb Saunders invites Reuven to live with him while Reuven's father recovers in the hospital. On the first day of July, Reuven moves into Danny's room.

SUMMARY: CHAPTER 12

The Saunderses treat Reuven like a member of the family. Danny's mother constantly heaps food on his plate, and Danny's sister jokingly teases the boys, calling them David and Jonathan, the inseparable biblical pair. Levi Saunders, Danny's brother, floats around the house, sickly and silent. Most perplexing, Danny's father broods constantly and occasionally breaks into tears for no apparent reason.

Danny and Reuven spend all their time together. They finally have the discussions they were unable to have during the busy school year. Danny patiently explains Freud to Reuven, and Reuven is astounded by the depth of Danny's knowledge and by the unsettling nature of Freud's theories.

During Reuven's visits to his father in the hospital, Mr. Malter speaks passionately about the need to build a Jewish homeland in Palestine. One morning, Reuven raises the topic of Zionism with Reb Saunders. Reb Saunders flies into a rage and screams that the activities of the secular Zionists are sacrilegious because it is profane to build a Jewish home in Israel before the arrival of the Messiah. Danny tells Reuven that if Reb Saunders knew of David Malter's Zionist beliefs, he would throw Reuven out of the house. Reuven never mentions the topic again in front of Reb Saunders, and Reb Saunders seems to forget the incident.

A few weeks later, while Reuven and Danny are studying in the library together, Danny confesses that one of the main reasons he worries about his brother Levi's health is that he wants Levi to take over his father's Hasidic dynasty so that he himself can study psychology. Danny remarks that the day he breaks this news to his father, he will need to have Reuven nearby for support. Reuven tries to change the subject by coyly mentioning Danny's sister. Danny quietly and peremptorily informs his friend that his sister was promised in marriage at the age of two, and the subject is never discussed between them again.

In August, Reuven and his father again go to their cottage near Peekskill, where his father recovers from his illness. That month, the United States drops atomic bombs on Japan, and the war with Japan ends. That fall, Reuven and Danny enter Hirsch College, and Danny begins to wear glasses.

ANALYSIS: CHAPTERS 11–12

In Chapter 11, Potok alternates between personal and historical tragedies, showing suffering to exist on both an individual and a societal level. The news of the German offensive is followed by news of Levi's illness. As the war in Europe intensifies, Danny falls sick with the flu. Roosevelt's death is followed by Reuven's fever, and David Malter's and Reb Saunders's illnesses. Then the terrible revelation of the concentration camps is followed by David Malter's heart attack. Although the historical tragedies do not directly cause the characters' illnesses, Potok links historical events to plot developments to demonstrate that World War II is not merely a backdrop for the novel, but an integral force in its characters' lives.

Following the news of President Roosevelt's death, Reuven directly states one of the novel's themes for the first time. He makes a connection between Roosevelt's death and Billy's blindness, saying that both events are "senseless" and "empty of meaning." Later in the chapter, the discovery of the concentration camps exponentially amplifies this feeling that the world is full of senseless suffering. The news of the Holocaust leads Reuven—as well as all other Jews—to question faith and religion.

Each of the novel's characters reacts differently to the challenge the Holocaust poses to believing in an all-knowing, ever-present God. Upon learning of the concentration camps, both David Malter and Reb Saunders weep for the loss of millions of European Jews. However, Reb Saunders accepts the Holocaust as God's will and, according to a strict and conservative interpretation of Jewish tradition, feels that Jews must wait for the Messiah to come to lead them to the Promised Land. Mr. Malter, on the other hand, argues that Jews cannot wait for God any longer; they must rebuild Jewry in America and found a Jewish state in Palestine. Although both men are deeply and profoundly pained by the mass extermination of the Jewish people, their political responses are radically different. Reb Saunders looks to Jewish tradition and its prophecy for comfort, while David Malter would rather create a new homeland than wait for the promises of a tradition—a tradition that the horror of the Holocaust calls into question.

In Chapter 12, Reuven's experience of living with the Malter family deepens his and our perception of Reb Saunders as a character. He relates that Reb Saunders randomly bursts into tears and walks as though there is "some kind of enormous burden on his shoulders." These mysterious moments suggest that Reb Saunders isn't as certain of his beliefs and actions as he appears to be.

Both Reuven and Danny share the burden of being Jews, of being part of the "chosen people" by virtue of their birth. In Danny's conversation with Reuven about feeling "trapped," Danny discusses how he also feels the burden of being chosen to succeed his father. He asks Reuven if he knows what it is like to feel trapped, and Reuven replies, somewhat hesitantly, that he does not. That Danny feels such a greater burden than Reuven suggests that the novel is more about conflict between fathers and sons than about conflict with religion and tradition. Such a perspective, however, is too simple, because Danny's problems with his father stem largely from issues of religion and tradition.

CHAPTER 13

SUMMARY: CHAPTER 13

> *"But the eye that blinks, that is something. A span of life is nothing. But the man who lives that span, he is something...."*
>
> *(See QUOTATIONS, p. 68)*

Danny and Reuven commence their studies at the Samson Raphael Hirsch Seminary and College, an Orthodox Jewish institution where the students' time is divided between Talmudic and secular education. Danny is placed in the highest Talmud class, taught by Rav Gershenson, and quickly becomes the leader of the small Hasid community at the school. Reuven is placed only one class below Danny. Danny, however, is primarily concerned with his psychological studies, and he is extremely distressed to learn that the psychology department at Hirsch only focuses on experimental psychology, and that the head of the department, Professor Appleman, criticizes Freud's methodologies. Reuven encourages Danny to talk with Professor Appleman about his concerns.

Reuven's father grows increasingly sickly and frail, but continues his passionate involvement in Zionist causes. He exhausts himself by speaking at rallies, raising money for the Jewish National Fund, and teaching adult education classes in Jewish subjects. When Reuven expresses concern about this father's health, Mr. Malter tells his son that he is trying to do something meaningful with his life before he dies, so that he will feel worthy of rest. Such blunt talk of death stings Reuven, and David Malter reassures his son that he will see a doctor for a checkup. The two continue talking, and eventually Reuven declares that he is firmly committed to becoming a rabbi. David Malter lovingly approves his son's decision, but warns him that American rabbis have a great responsibility to educate newly curious Jews in the aftermath of World War II.

On a Friday afternoon, Reuven goes to the college library and looks through some texts on experimental psychology. He begins to understand Danny's frustration with his studies. However, a few days later, Danny tells him that after an hour-long talk with Professor Appleman, he has come to respect Appleman's opinions. Danny also mentions that Appleman suggested he find someone to help him learn mathematics, so Reuven agrees to tutor Danny.

The Hirsch student body becomes polarized into two starkly opposed factions: those who support the Zionists on one side and those who oppose the establishment of a Jewish state in Palestine on the other. Day by day, tension grows between the groups. One night, Reuven's father delivers an influential speech at a Madison Square Garden rally in support of the Zionist cause. The day after the rally, Danny avoids Reuven entirely, and the next day, he secretly tells Reuven that his father has forbidden him to see or speak to Reuven, on account of David Malter's Zionist beliefs. This is extremely painful for Reuven, but when he denounces Reb Saunders as a fanatic to his father, his father responds, "the fanaticism of men like Reb Saunders kept us alive for two thousand years of exile." Despite his father's words, Reuven remains deeply angry with Reb Saunders and sad that his relationship with Danny appears to be over.

ANALYSIS: CHAPTER 13

Chapter 13 introduces a series of conflicts between tradition and modernity. We see the novel's characters trying to preserve their traditional beliefs as they encounter the modern world they inhabit. Danny is the first character to deal with this conflict. His reaction to

Hirsch's psychology department humorously introduces the inevitable conflict between Danny's upbringing and the world of modern intellectualism he wants to enter. Danny has always seen psychology as a way of breaking away from his tradition, but we already have seen that he only mastered Freud after using the same method of studying he uses when reading the Talmud. Danny's arduous intellectual upbringing emphasized theory and commentary, but left him ill prepared for the modern world's emphasis on scientific analysis and experimentation. Danny's frustration demonstrates that, despite his efforts to break away from his tradition, he is unquestionably a product of that tradition.

The most significant conflict between tradition and modernity occurs over the question of a Jewish state. As the previous two chapters make clear, traditionalists like Reb Saunders believe that, despite the tragedy Jews have experienced, they must continue to observe scripture and wait for the coming of the Messiah. The other position, held by David Malter, argues that modern Jewry must give meaning to the horrible tragedy of the Holocaust by establishing a modern Jewish state. The climax of this conflict between anti-Zionism and Zionism is Reb Saunders's prohibiting Danny from seeing or speaking to Reuven following David Malter's speech in support of Zionism. Yet, at the end of the chapter, David Malter's defense of Reb Saunders's fanaticism underscores the complexity of the conflict. The conflict between tradition and modernity is something all the characters must struggle with individually, and all Jews must struggle with as a culture. No character simply chooses one side or the other; the reconciliation of tradition with modernity is a process of balance and compromise.

David Malter's speech at Madison Square Garden implies a certain kind of fanaticism that parallels Reb Saunders's zealous behavior, including his refusal to speak with his son. Just as the rabbi is fanatically opposed to the modern State of Israel, so too is David Malter fanatically committed to its establishment—even at the expense of his health. We again realize that on a personal level, these two fathers are not as different as they appear to be.

When Danny worries about Professor Appleman, Reuven displays his belief in open verbal communication by suggesting that Danny go talk to his professor. Reuven's advice is a product of his upbringing, in which his father has lovingly educated him using the spoken word. Reuven equates silence with loneliness, a lack of communication, and the elimination of learning. In his thoughts, he pities Danny for having to deal with his father's inexplicable, "bizarre silence," which Reuven believes must be "torturing [Danny's] soul."

In David Malter's speech to Reuven about the importance of giving his life meaning, he refers to the image of the eye, which suggests the centrality of the eye—and by extension, the centrality of vision—to human life. Furthermore, the fact that he uses an eye not as a symbol of looking but as an example of something to be looked at introduces some complexity to the novel's exploration of vision. Here, David Malter suggests that vision operates in two directions: the eye functions both to send and to receive information. He implies that vision—seeing the world—is a reciprocal process, a two-way street of giving and receiving.

CHAPTER 14

SUMMARY: CHAPTER 14

For the remainder of their first year at college, Danny and Reuven have no contact with each other, and Reuven is furious at Reb Saunders. Meanwhile, Danny's father has intensified his anti-Zionist activity, and tensions increase between the opposing factions at the college. Reuven's pain at losing Danny's friendship leads him to do poorly on his exams. The summer provides little respite: July and August are marked by horrible violent events in Palestine, then David Malter is forced to cut short the annual vacation in Peekskill to deal with pressing Zionist matters. When the new semester begins in September, Reuven decides that he wants nothing more to do with Danny Saunders, but his resolve is challenged by the fact that he now shares Rav Gershenson's Talmud class with Danny.

Rav Gershenson is a gentle, wise old scholar. His Talmud class is rigorous, and, of course, Danny is his star pupil. Danny and Gershenson frequently have lengthy discussions in class that remind Reuven of the Talmud sessions he and Danny used to have with Reb Saunders. Reuven feels comfortable with the material, and when he is called on in early October, Gershenson is pleased with his response. But for some reason, Gershenson refuses to call on him again. By the middle of October, Reuven is the only student who has not been called more than once and he is perplexed.

In November, the United Nations votes in favor of the Partition Plan to establish a Jewish state, and Reb Saunders accelerates his anti-Zionist activities. His supporters plaster anti-Zionist leaflets all over Hirsch College, and fistfights nearly break out among the students. Reuven almost screams at the anti-Zionist protestors, but stays silent. As the first semester ends, Reuven receives straight A's—even in Rav Gershenson's class—and Reuven's father continues to work tirelessly in support of the UN decision. During Reuven's winter break, his father collapses at a Jewish National Fund meeting, suffering a second heart attack. In school, Danny brushes up against Reuven in a gesture of sympathy, but remains unable to speak to him.

David Malter is hospitalized for over a month, and Reuven lives at home alone, feeling incredibly lonely. He deals with the newfound silence in his apartment by diving ferociously into his Talmudic studies. Although Gershenson has not called on him for several months, he becomes convinced that he will be called upon for one particularly difficult passage that none of the students can understand, so he prepares an especially intense analysis.

As Reuven expected, Rav Gershenson finally calls on him to clarify the difficult passage, and Reuven finds himself dominating the class for several days. Although he has figured out how to apply his father's critical methods to resolve the text's internal contradictions, he refrains from employing these controversial methods in front of the class because he thinks that Rav Gershenson would not approve. Instead, he gives an extraordinarily thorough interpretation using traditional methods like the ones Reb Saunders would use with Danny.

After class, Rav Gershenson detains Reuven and asks him how his father might have resolved the passage's contradictions. Reuven explains how his father would have reconstructed the text to make sense of it. Rav Gershenson is clearly impressed and praises both Reuven and his father. He says that he is not personally opposed to these controversial techniques but tells Reuven that he must never use them in his class. Afterward, Reuven looks for Rav Gershenson's name in the school library's card catalog, but does not find it. He realizes that Gershenson cannot publish, because if he expressed his belief in controversial Talmud scholarship, he would not be allowed to teach at the conservative college. Reuven realizes that his father's controversial writings are the reason he is not teaching at Hirsch, even though he is a brilliant scholar.

ANALYSIS: CHAPTER 14

In this chapter, Reuven has neither Danny nor Reb Saunders in his life, and after his father's heart attack, he feels entirely alone. Rav Gershenson functions as a substitute for all these characters, filling a void in Reuven's life. Therefore, by observing Rav Gershenson and what he means to Reuven, we get a better sense of what Reb Saunders, Danny Saunders, and Reuven's father mean to Reuven.

Since he is Reuven's Talmud teacher, Rav Gershenson functions most obviously as a surrogate for Reb Saunders. In Rav Gershenson's class, Reuven is given insight into the Talmud, which he loves, and he is indirectly able to interact with Danny. Like Reb Saunders, Rav Gershenson uses silence as a tool of instruction. Yet Rav Gershenson's silence seems different from Reb Saunders's harsh refusal to speak to Danny. Rav Gershenson's silence is gentle, it occurs in the context of classroom learning, and it serves to highlight a student's lack of knowledge.

Rav Gershenson's patient, loving approach to learning also echoes David Malter's education of Reuven. Reuven himself makes this connection, commenting, "he taught Talmud the way my father did." After his father's heart attack, Reuven finds solace in his Talmudic studies. Studying for Rav Gershenson helps Reuven feel connected to his father, as he applies, celebrates, and reaps the rewards of his father's patient teachings.

More subtly, Rav Gershenson's class serves as a substitute for Danny in Reuven's life. We understand exactly what Danny means to Reuven by learning how Reuven compensates for his absence. Danny has given Reuven a new perspective. Through Danny, Reuven has crossed into a world so similar to, yet so different from, the world where he always felt comfortable. Danny has broadened Reuven's worldview and enabled Reuven to look at the world from multiple viewpoints. In Reuven's Talmudic study, we see how Reuven's relationship with Danny has initiated Reuven's maturation. Reuven says, "I worked carefully and methodically, using everything my father had taught me and a lot of things I now was able to teach myself." His father taught him the tools to learn far beyond the bounds of his upbringing, and Danny is the one who showed Reuven other ways of studying the Talmud.

The strength of Reuven's analysis, which impresses Rav Gershenson, is its breadth the multiplicity of voices he includes. Reuven learned depth from his father, but from Danny, he learned to approach a problem from several different perspectives. In the end,

Reuven does not even use his father's methodology during his in-class explication, but instead uses Reb Saunders's approach. From the start of his friendship with Danny, Reuven learned to look beyond superficial appearances, doubt his initial impressions, and search for multiple ways of looking at a situation. In Rav Gershenson's class, we see how these lessons have impacted Reuven's life.

Throughout the novel, Reuven criticizes Reb Saunder's silent treatment of Danny. He also finds unbearable the silence Reb Saunders has imposed between Reuven and Danny. At the beginning of this chapter, Reuven says that he frequently met eyes with Danny, "but [their] lips exchanged nothing." This comment implies the pain Danny's silence is causing Reuven, and it also suggests that Reuven believes wordless interactions are meaningless. Yet the silence Reuven experiences throughout this entire chapter results in his most accomplished scholarship. Also, after Reuven restrains himself from shouting at the anti-Zionists, he says, "I was grateful for that silence." He sees that words as well as silence can hurt and cause suffering, and he is glad that he restrained himself. Reuven is growing to understand that the difference between silence and speech is not as clear-cut as he initially believed.

Chapters 15–16

Summary: Chapter 15
In March, David Malter returns from the hospital and Reuven is elated to have his father home. At school, Rav Gershenson now calls on him regularly, and Reuven is always ready with expert answers. Danny continues to ignore Reuven, and Reuven finally comes to accept Danny's silence.

As fighting in Palestine increases, Reuven and his Zionist classmates intensify their efforts, even volunteering to load supply trucks with military gear to be shipped overseas. In April, David Malter wistfully tells Reuven that he had been selected to be a delegate at the Zionist General Council in Palestine the coming summer. However, following his heart attack, he no longer will be able to attend. In May, the State of Israel is born, and Reuven and his father weep with joy. The Arabs immediately attack the young nation, and as they invade, David Malter again becomes distracted and unsettled. In June, the students at Hirsch learn that a recent Hirsch graduate was killed during the fighting. The college holds a memorial assembly, and all anti-Zionist activity at Hirsch immediately ceases.

Reuven receives straight A's for his sophomore year, passes a quiet July in sweltering New York, and a calm August with his father at their cottage. In September, he begins his third year at college and chooses philosophy as his major. David Malter gradually resumes his teaching, and then, a few months later, his Zionist activities. That spring, after Israel has secured the upper hand, Reb Saunders's anti-Zionist activities appear to end. Soon after, Danny approaches Reuven in the lunchroom, and, with a smile on his face, asks for Reuven's help with math.

SUMMARY: CHAPTER 16

After not speaking for more than two years, Reuven and Danny talk about the silence that existed between them. Reuven asks Danny how he can possibly bear the silence between him and his father, and Danny replies that he has learned to live with it. Reuven also expresses his dislike for Reb Saunders and remarks that Danny has lost weight. Danny says that his eyes have been bothering him. That night, Reuven discusses Reb Saunders's imposed silence with his father. David Malter cryptically remarks, "What a price to pay for a soul," but refuses to explain any further.

Danny and Reuven resume their regular weekday meetings, and also begin having dazzling disputes in class that please Rav Gershenson. Outside of class, Danny reveals that he resigned himself to the experimental methods of psychology and has begun to see the shortcomings in Freud's work. Nevertheless, he still does not want to become an experimental psychologist. Instead, he has decided to go into clinical psychology, which combines experimental hypotheses with therapeutic work with human patients. Also, Danny has applied to doctoral programs in psychology. He informs Reuven that he is waiting until the day of his smicha—his Rabbinic ordination—to break the news to his father.

That June, Reuven attends Danny's sister's wedding and sees Reb Saunders for the first time in more than two years. Since Reuven last saw him, Danny's father appears to have aged a great deal. Due to the crowd of people at the wedding, Reuven is unable to speak to Reb Saunders, but he does not mind the lack of communication with the rabbi, whom he still dislikes intensely. Later that summer, in July, Reuven visits Danny's house and goes up to Reb Saunders's study. Danny's father says he is very happy to see Reuven and asks why he has not been coming over on Saturday afternoons to study Talmud. Reuven answers that he has

SUMMARY & ANALYSIS

been studying with his own father, but Reb Saunders asks him if he could come over one Saturday anyway. Though Reuven says he will try, he has no intention of honoring Reb Saunders's request. After Reb Saunders says nothing about Zionism or about the silence he imposed between Danny and Reuven, Reuven finds he likes the old man even less than before.

ANALYSIS: CHAPTERS 15–16

Chapter 15 is brief and serves mostly to advance the plot. We learn about the creation of the State of Israel, the collapse of the tension over Zionism at Hirsch, and the resumption of Danny and Reuven's friendship. Once again, we see a relationship between personal and historical events. Tension only disappears at Hirsch after the fighting in Israel results in the death of a Hirsch alumnus. Throughout the entire novel, Potok carefully shows how the events that affect individual Jewish characters are inseparable from the larger events in Jewish history. The fighting in Israel touches the Jewish students' lives, and it underscores the fact that tradition and modernity will always be forced into contact and conflict with one another.

It is important to note that Reuven imposes silence on Reb Saunders, refusing to listen to the old man or to come over for Shabbat. Again, we see that silence means many different things in the novel; it is not only a cruel punishment inflicted by Reb Saunders.

When David Malter refuses to explain Reb Saunders's behavior to Reuven, he too mimics Reb Saunders's silent way of interacting with his son. During this moment of refusal, Reuven notes that his father's "eyes were dark." This description has two symbolic meanings. By denying his son information, David Malter is clouding his son's vision. From this point of view, his dark eyes reflect the darkness and the lack of perspective that he is imposing on Reuven. Also, Reuven's description shows that eyes are not just a tool for receiving information, but also a tool for displaying information. Reuven's father's eyes here reflect his internal state. It is a complex moment that implies that vision is a two-way process of both sending and receiving information.

Once Danny and Reuven resume their friendship, the lessons they have learned during their time spent apart become clearer. For example, even though Reuven continues to help Danny with math, something Danny would not be able to grasp on his own, Reuven tells Danny "it [is] about time he helped himself with graphs." During the boys' period of isolation, Reuven learned that his friendship with Danny had enabled him to be a stronger person, and he realized he was able to help himself. At the same time, we also are reminded of other ways in which Danny and Reuven give one another things that each would not be able to get on his own. In a touching exchange, Danny says to Reuven that he can't believe Reuven is going to be a rabbi, and Reuven responds that he can't believe Danny is going to be a psychologist. Potok here points out the almost yin-yang relationship between Danny and Reuven. In many ways, each is the opposite of the other, yet they also fit together perfectly.

CHAPTER 17

SUMMARY: CHAPTER 17

In the fall, Reuven and Danny begin their final year of college. One day, Reuven makes what he thinks is an innocent joke about hearing silence. Danny responds that Reuven is being more insightful than he realizes. Danny explains that he has begun to hear silence—he listens to it and hears it talking to him. He also tells Reuven that he cannot start dating because a wife has already been chosen for him.

Reuven attends Levi Saunders's Bar Mitzvah in October. The next day, Levi becomes violently ill and is taken to the hospital. Reuven tells his father about Levi's illness. He also reveals to his father that Danny is panicking about the illness because he has been relying on his brother to take over the dynasty. David Malter encourages Reuven to speak with Danny about how he plans to break this news to his father. David Malter also enigmatically reveals more about the custom of raising a child in silence, saying it is an old Hasidic tradition that is used to teach children compassion. But again, he refuses to give Reuven any specific information.

The following week, when Danny tells Reuven that he is applying to Harvard, Berkeley, and Columbia for a fellowship in psychology, Reuven urges him to figure out how he will tell his father. Danny tries to brush aside Reuven's concerns, but soon realizes that his father will inevitably see the mail from the schools to which he has applied. He becomes panicked, and Reuven urges Danny to come over and talk to David Malter. That evening, Reuven's father cautions Danny that he must carefully consider all that his decision entails, including breaking off his pre-arranged marriage. He also warns Danny that he must thoughtfully plan exactly what he will say to Reb Saunders on the day of the confrontation. Before Danny leaves, David Malter asks him if he can, in fact, hear silence. Danny replies that he can, and asks Reuven's father if he understands the way his father has raised him. David Malter refuses to explain the matter to either Danny or Reuven, saying it is a private matter between Danny and his father.

Danny receives acceptance letters from all three schools he applied to. Though Reb Saunders has obviously seen the return addresses on the envelopes, he has not approached Danny about them. Danny decides to go to Columbia, but he is still too afraid to broach the subject with his father. While discussing his dilemma with Reuven, Danny mentions that Reb Saunders has been asking again why Reuven has not come over for a Shabbat Talmud session.

In the months that follow, Reb Saunders, through Danny, continues to drop hints that he would like Reuven to come over some Shabbat afternoon. Because of his dislike for the rabbi, Reuven continues to ignore the requests. Later that spring, Danny tells Reuven that Reb Saunders has made the special request that Reuven come over on the first or second day of Passover. That night, Reuven tells his father that Reb Saunders has been asking to see him. David Malter becomes quite angry with his son, saying he should speak with Reb Saunders if Reb Saunders wishes him to do so. He points out that Reb Saunders wants to use Reuven to talk to Danny. Reuven quickly calls Danny and tells him he will come over the following Sunday, during Passover.

ANALYSIS: CHAPTER 17

Reb Saunders's silence continues to be the central mystery of *The Chosen*. Potok uses Reb Saunders's silence as a literary device that allows us to empathize with both Reuven and Danny. By not explaining the meaning of Reb Saunders's silence, the novel imposes a kind of silence on the reader. Because we are confused and frustrated about the meaning of silence, we can better understand Reuven and Danny's frustration with Reb Saunders's mysterious method of parenting.

There are many other instances of silence within the novel, which reinforce the complexity and subtlety of the relationship between silence and communication. When Danny reveals that he has learned to hear silence, he strengthens the idea of silence as a means of communication. Danny's paradoxical statement perplexes Reuven, because it implies that a lack of sound need not entail a lack of knowledge and information. Danny's statement shows us that silence is a complex concept, that it can have form and function, and that it can affect a person as much as words.

Furthermore, in this chapter, David Malter continues the silence he has been imposing on Reuven. Leaving Reuven bewildered, he again refuses to explain Reb Saunders's behavior. At the end of the chapter, Reuven realizes that by refusing to visit the Saunders household, he himself has been imposing a silence upon Reb Saunders. Reuven has been preventing Reb Saunders from communicating with Danny the only way he is able to, through Reuven.

The conversation between Danny and David Malter at the Malter's apartment is the first time since Reuven's hospitalization that all three have had a conversation in the same room. This interaction disrupts the binary relationships that Potok has carefully set up over the course of the novel. Up to this point, David Malter and Reuven have been a pair, set in opposition to the other father-son pair, Danny and Reb Saunders. Danny and Reuven are also a pair, set in opposition to the figures of David Malter and Reb Saunders. Here, the boundaries between the pairs collapse as Danny—for the first time since Reuven's hospitalization—talks directly with Reuven's father. This collapse in the book's boundaries foreshadows the crucial change that occurs in the following chapter, during the book's climax.

David Malter reveals a surprising facet of his character during his conversation with Danny. As he talks to Danny about silence, his response reflects astonishment at—perhaps even respect for—Danny's ability. David Malter tells Danny that Danny's father will want him to raise his own children in same way. David Malter's response to Danny's decision has a different tone than the disgust he displayed earlier, when he could not understand why the Hasidim felt like they had to carry the burdens of the world. As we shall see in the coming chapter, David Malter's opinions of Hasidism are complex and differ from how they first appeared.

CHAPTER 18

SUMMARY: CHAPTER 18

*"It makes us aware of how frail and tiny we are and of
how much we must depend upon the Master of the
Universe."*

(See QUOTATIONS, p. 69)

On the afternoon of the first day of Passover, Reuven goes over to
the Saunderses' house, where Danny greets him. Full of fear,
Danny leads Reuven up to his father's third floor study. Inside,
everything is exactly as Reuven remembers it, except Reb Saunders himself, who looks haggard and stooped with suffering. He
greets Reuven and makes some small talk. When Reuven says he
plans to be a rabbi after graduation, Reb Saunders stiffens as
though in pain. In a soft voice, he remarks that after graduation,
Danny and Reuven will go "different ways." Danny's mouth falls
open in shock: he and Reuven realize that Reb Saunders knows
about Danny's plans not to become a rabbi.

Reb Saunders continues, talking to Danny through Reuven,
never once looking at his son. He explains why he raised the
Danny the way he did. From a very early age, he saw that Danny
had an unbelievably brilliant mind, but possessed little soul. As a
young boy, Danny felt no compassion for the suffering of others,
no empathy, no sense of mercy. Reb Saunders tells the story of his
brother, who forsook Jewish observance in favor of intellectual
pursuits and then died in the gas chambers of Auschwitz. He
explains that only knowledge of the immense suffering in the
world can redeem one's soul.

Reb Saunders reveals that the silence he imposed upon Danny
was a way to teach him compassion, to teach him to feel the suffering of others. His own father raised him that way. Reb Saunders
learned through silence to turn inward, to feel his own pain and, in
doing so, to suffer for his people. He says that bearing this burden of
suffering is a fundamental part of being a tzaddik.

In America, Reb Saunders explains, he could not prevent Danny
from his ravenous pursuit of knowledge. He decided to raise Danny in
silence, understanding that it would drive Danny away from becoming
a rabbi, because he felt it was most important that Danny's "soul would
be the soul of a tzaddik no matter what he did with his life."

Danny's father finishes by telling Reuven that he and David Malter have been a blessing to Reb Saunders. He says he knew Reuven and his father both possessed good, deep souls, and he thanks God for sending both of them to Danny at a time when he was ready to rebel. In conclusion, he announces that he does not care what profession Danny chooses—he knows now that his son has the soul of a tzaddik, and "he will be a tzaddik for the world" no matter what job he holds. Reb Saunders turns to Danny. Speaking quietly, he asks his son if he will shave off his beard and earlocks for graduate school; Danny nods that he will. He asks if Danny will continue to observe the Ten Commandments; Danny nods again. Stuttering, Reb Saunders then asks Reuven to forgive him for the silence he imposed between him and Danny. His voice breaks, and he turns to Danny, asking his son to forgive him for the pain his style of parenting caused. Then, his shoulders stooped and his face full of grief, he shuffles out of the room. Danny bursts into tears. Reuven, also crying, tries to comfort him. Afterward, the two boys walk for hours in total silence.

When Reuven returns home, he and his father discuss what Reb Saunders said. David Malter says that a father has a right to raise his son however he sees fit, but that he does not like the way Danny was raised. He tells Reuven that he is glad not to be a tzaddik and not to have the burden of raising his son as a tzaddik. A few weeks later, Reb Saunders announces to his congregation that Danny will study psychology, thereby implying that he is transferring inheritance of the tzaddikate to Levi. Reb Saunders also withdraws his promise to the family of the girl Danny was supposed to marry.

Both Reuven and Danny graduate summa cum laude from Hirsch College. One evening in the fall, Danny, now without beard or earlocks, comes over to the Malters' apartment to say goodbye before he moves to an apartment in Manhattan, near Columbia University. Danny mentions that he and his father now speak regularly to each other. David Malter asks Danny if, in the future, he will raise his son in silence. Danny replies that he will, unless he can find another way to teach his son to have the soul of a tzaddik. Danny promises to return on Saturdays to study Talmud, and Reuven watches as Danny turns and walks away, his metal-capped shoes tapping on the sidewalk.

ANALYSIS: CHAPTER 18

We shook hands and I watched him walk quickly away,
tall, lean, bent forward with eagerness and hungry for
the future, his metal capped shoes tapping against the
sidewalk.

(See QUOTATIONS, p. 70)

Chapter 18 resolves the conflict between Danny and his father that resulted from Danny's unexpressed desire to break away from his culture and tradition. The chapter also reveals the meaning of the novel's mysterious instances of silence. In the novel's resolution, Potok radically alters our perspective on all the characters, and on Reb Saunders in particular. We learn the surprising news that Reb Saunders knows of and does not object to Danny's decision not to assume his legacy. As Reb Saunders tearfully explains why he raised Danny the way he did, we learn the same lessons that Reuven and Danny have been learning throughout the novel: people are not always how they initially appear, and we cannot dismiss that which we do not understand. By revealing information to us in the same order he learned it himself, Reuven narrates his story in a way that makes us experience the lessons he and Danny learned as they experienced them. We therefore empathize with Reuven and Danny's newfound awareness.

At first, Reb Saunders's silence toward Danny seemed a cruel punishment that indicated he did not care about his son. Now, we realize that Reb Saunders's silence reflects how much he cares about Danny—through silence, he has taught Danny to find his own soul. Therefore, we realize that Reb Saunders's goal was noble, even though his methods were harsh. He chose to cultivate Danny's emotions and sympathy for others by treating him with silence, knowing it would turn him away from the tzaddikate. Reb Saunders wants his son to have the essence of a tzaddik, however he chooses to live his life.

David Malter's reaction to Reb Saunders's parenting also tempers our understanding of Mr. Malter and Reb Saunders. Instead of condemning Reb Saunders's actions, Mr. Malter merely acknowledges that Reb Saunders had no choice. It is an acknowledgement of the difference between his situation and that of Reb Saunders, and of a respect for those differences. Like the other characters in the book, David Malter too has been educated and broadened by Reuven's relationship with Danny.

Danny's experience with his father's silence parallels Reuven's brush with blindness. Reuven's injury forced him to reevaluate and deepen his understanding of the world. Through suffering, Reuven gained empathy for others. The threat of blindness, of lack of perception, gave Reuven a greater appreciation for his abilities of perception. For Danny, enduring his father's silence was a similar experience of stifled perception. When Danny was surrounded by silence, he learned to turn inward, to examine his own soul, to feel empathy for others, and to feel suffering.

For Reuven and for us, the meaning of silence has been mysterious throughout the novel. Moments of silence in the novel alternate between being terrible and welcome, cruel and warm. Always, silence leads the characters to introspection. Potok emphasizes the importance of words, communication, and conversation, but he equally emphasizes silence and its profound broadening effect. To underscore the effectiveness of silence, after the talk with Reb Saunders, Reuven and Danny walk "in silence ... saying more ... than with a lifetime of words."

It is notable that *The Chosen*'s climax—Reb Saunders's conversation with Danny and Reuven—involves a trio of characters. Most of the novel's action concerns pairs of characters: either Danny and Reuven, or Danny and Reb Saunders, or Reuven and Mr. Malter. Mr. Malter and Danny, and Reb Saunders and Reuven also have moments of conversation. Even the previous meetings between Reb Saunders, Danny, and Reuven were not really trios, because Danny had to leave the room for earnest conversation to take place. By disrupting the normal two-person structure of interaction in the novel, the novel's climax highlights the way Reb Saunders's words disrupt the seemingly rigid world of Danny's Hasidic life. Reuven and Danny have been learning that the world is full of surprises, that if they keep an open mind they will discover new ways to look at the world. This lesson is reinforced by the presence of a trio in the world that up until this point has been dominated by pairs.

To highlight the way Reuven and Danny's perception of the world has been broadened, the novel's final passage places heavy emphasis on sight and sound. Reuven watches Danny walk away and listens to Danny's shoes tap on the sidewalk. In its focus on sight and sound, the novel's closing reminds us of the way Reuven and Danny learned about the world through near-blindness and silence. Because it describes the separation of Danny and Reuven, the passage also highlights the importance their friendship held to their growth. Their empathy for human beings and for each other results from their reciprocal interaction, from the way they complement, parallel, and contrast with and teach each other. Reb Saunders acknowledges this same fact when he thanks God for bringing Reuven into Danny's life.

IMPORTANT QUOTATIONS EXPLAINED

1. *I stood in that room for a long time, watching the sunlight
    and listening to the sounds on the street outside. I stood
    there, tasting the room and the sunlight and the sounds, and
    thinking of the long hospital ward. . . . I wondered if little
    Mickey had ever seen sunlight come though the windows of
    a front room apartment. . . . Somehow everything had
    changed. I had spent five days in a hospital and the world
    around seemed sharpened now and pulsing with life.*

This passage occurs in Chapter 5, after Reuven has returned home
from the hospital. His eye accident and brush with blindness taught
him about the fragility of his senses. In this passage, Reuven shows
he has developed a deep appreciation for the gift of perception as he
describes "watching," "listening to," and "tasting" the world
around him.

Not only has Reuven's accident heightened his physical awareness of the world around him; it has also heightened his perception
of the world's suffering and complexity. In the hospital, he encoun-
tered people in painful and cruel situations. Displaying a new sense
of empathy and compassion, Reuven worries about Mickey, the boy
who has been in the hospital his whole life. Reuven's eyes have been
opened to the injustice and suffering in the world. As a result,
Reuven appreciates the quality of his own circumstances—of his
sunny apartment—which are superior to those of the dingy hospital
ward. Throughout the novel, Potok portrays the development of
compassion for the suffering of others as a crucial element of maturity.

Reuven also first meets Danny when Danny visits him in the hospital, and Reuven's conversations with Danny are equally important to Reuven's heightened awareness of the world. Danny
contributes to Reuven's improved sense of perception by defying all
of Reuven's preconceived assumptions about Hasidic Judaism.
Reuven's focus on his physical senses in this passage also emphasizes
the importance of looking deeper than a first glance. In order to
show how Reuven's way of seeing others has changed, Potok

65

stresses the way Reuven's apartment, something he has known all his life, seems a new place. In this passage, Reuven reveals the after-effects of his hospital experience: his perception, on all levels, has been broadened and deepened by his accident, by the suffering he witnesses, and by his interaction with Danny Saunders.

2. *"We are commanded to study His Torah! We are
    commanded to sit in the light of the Presence! It is for this
    that we were created! . . . Not the world, but the people of
    Israel!"*

In this passage, taken from Reb Saunders's inflammatory speech in
Chapter 7, Reb Saunders expresses his feelings about what it means
for Jews to be the "Chosen People" by comparing their duties to
those of non-Jews. To be a Jew, he argues, is to accept a destiny and
a set of responsibilities that Jews receive by virtue of their birth. By
dismissing the non-Jewish world around him, Reb Saunders implies
that a truly faithful Jew should retreat to an exclusively Jewish community, immerse himself in Jewish study, and pay little attention to
anything in the outside world. For Reb Saunders, "the world"—
anything beyond the boundaries of his community, any literature
beyond the boundaries of conservative Jewish tradition—is base.
Even when world events overlap with Jewish concerns—such as the
horrible discovery of the slaughter of European Jews in the Holocaust—Reb Saunders chooses to focus inward, on his own community, and on his own sense of suffering.

However, Reb Saunders's definition of the obligations of Jews
seems to shift by the end of the novel. His acceptance of Danny's
decision to become a professional psychologist suggests that he recognizes one can maintain ties with the outside world and be observant of one's faith.

QUOTATIONS

3. *"What does it mean to have to suffer so much if our lives are
    nothing more than the blink of an eye? ... I learned a long
    time ago, Reuven, that a blink of an eye in itself is nothing.
    But the eye that blinks, that is something. A span of life is
    nothing. But the man who lives that span, he is
    something...."*

Explaining his relentless Zionist activism, David Malter speaks
these words to Reuven in Chapter 13. In this complex passage,
Potok ties together several thematic elements. David Malter
emphasizes the prevalence of suffering, then explains that awareness of the world's suffering makes a person empathize with others and therefore appreciate all life and every detail of God's
creation. His point is that although we may believe "the blink of
an eye is nothing," we should appreciate the eye's mere existence,
and the blink's mere existence. It is significant that David Malter
uses the eye as an image in making his point. Potok intersperses
eye imagery throughout *The Chosen* to symbolize perception of
the world and of one's own soul. Furthermore, David Malter's
description of observing the eye implies that perception is a reciprocal, two-way process. In David Malter's opinion, deeper
appreciation of life leads to a sense of obligation to fill one's life
with meaning and make the world a better place.

The passage also contrasts with Reb Saunders's diatribe in
Chapter 7, excerpted in the quotation above. The differences
between the two passages point to the differences between the
two fathers. Unlike Reb Saunders, David Malter speaks in a gentle tone, explaining rather than proclaiming. David Malter's tone
is that of a sympathetic teacher rather than a harsh leader.
Whereas Reb Saunders argues for Jews to retreat passively into
study and believes that meaning is given to life at birth, David
Malter believes life is not given meaning at birth. He argues that
a person fills life with meaning along the way. Whereas Reb Saunders suggests that Jews are passively chosen for duty, David
Malter believes that Jews have an obligation to actively choose a
noble path and to make a difference in the world.

THE CHOSEN ✹ 69

4. *"[My father] taught me with silence...to look into myself, to
    find my own strength, to walk around inside myself in
    company with my soul.... One learns of the pain of others
    by suffering one's own pain ... by turning inside oneself....
    It makes us aware of how frail and tiny we are and of how
    much we must depend upon the Master of the Universe."*

Using Reuven as an intermediary, Reb Saunders speaks these words
to Danny in Chapter 18. In his speech, Reb Saunders finally reveals
his reasons for imposing silence upon Danny for so many years. Up
to this point, Reuven has tacitly assumed that Reb Saunders's silence
was a cruel punishment that reflected emotional distance and a lack
of love. Here, Reb Saunders explains that his silence has very noble,
loving intentions: he wanted Danny to find his own soul.

We see that silence, as Reb Saunders intended it, functions very
similarly to Reuven's experience in the hospital. After his eye accident, Reuven developed a heightened appreciation for his physical
senses. Furthermore, after witnessing the suffering of others,
Reuven developed a sense of empathy for others. His experience
was painful but life-changing. Reb Saunders describes the experience of being raised in silence along similar lines. Silence, he argues,
engenders introspection, creates humility and empathy, deepens
one's appreciation for life, and affirms one's sense of commitment to
others and to God.

5. *"We shook hands and I watched him walk quickly away,*
    tall, lean, bent forward with eagerness and hungry for the
    future, his metal capped shoes tapping against the sidewalk.
    Then he turned into Lee Avenue and was gone."

This farewell scene is the final passage of *The Chosen*. Danny is
about to leave the neighborhood to attend graduate school, and by
ending with an emphasis on the fact that Danny "was gone,"
Reuven reminds us that Danny is leaving, finally, the boundaries of
his community. Danny has rejected the destiny that was chosen for
him and has chosen his own path instead.

Because Reuven emphasizes his subjective perception of Danny's
departure, the passage is as much about Reuven as about Danny.
Reuven mentions four of his senses in this description: touch (shak-
ing hands), vision (watching Danny walk away), taste ("hungry for
the future"), and hearing (Danny's shoes tapping). This emphasis on
all types of perception underscores the way Reuven is not only
acutely aware of the world around him, he also experiences the
world in multiple ways. This multisensory perspective reflects the
way Reuven's perception has broadened as a result of his friendship
with Danny—just as Danny's has deepened as result of his friendship with Reuven.

When reading *The Chosen*, we are tempted to see Danny's conflict with his father as the only significant aspect of the novel. Yet
Reuven is an equally significant character, and it is important to
notice the way he too develops. The central story of *The Chosen* is
not the story of Danny and his father, but the story of two friends
and how they affect each other's lives. For this reason, Potok closes
the novel by emphasizing Danny and Reuven's friendship and,
through his emphasis on senses and perception, demonstrating how
their view of the world has changed.

KEY FACTS

FULL TITLE
The Chosen

AUTHOR
Chaim Potok

TYPE OF WORK
Novel

GENRE
Bildungsroman; Jewish-American Literature

LANGUAGE
English

TIME AND PLACE WRITTEN
1960–1967, in Philadelphia, Israel, and Brooklyn

DATE OF FIRST PUBLICATION
1967

PUBLISHER
Simon and Schuster

NARRATOR
The Chosen is narrated by Reuven Malter, who reflects several years after the events of the novel on his coming-of-age in Brooklyn.

POINT OF VIEW
Reuven Malter, the narrator, speaks in the first-person. He explains events in chronological order, adjusting his perspective over the course of the novel to reflect his increasing maturity. Reuven's narration is not omniscient, as he does not know what others are thinking or feeling. Instead, he reveals Reuven's observations of others' behavior and analyzes other characters' thoughts and emotions.

TONE

Reuven is an introspective, highly intellectual young man. As a result, he is rarely quick to judge others, and usually spends time considering multiple perspectives, trying to be as thoughtful and open-minded as possible. These qualities only improve as his relationship with Danny alters the way he looks at the world. It is important to note that for the majority of the novel, Reuven is very quick to judge Reb Saunders and rather harsh in his judgment. Only at the very end of the novel does he learn that he has not been seeing the complexity of Reb Saunders's character.

TENSE

Past

SETTINGS (TIME)

Early summer, 1944 to fall, 1950

SETTING (PLACE)

The neighborhood of Williamsburg in Brooklyn, New York

PROTAGONISTS

Reuven Malter and Danny Saunders

MAJOR CONFLICT

Danny's struggle between his family and religious obligations, and his desire to become a psychologist is the novel's central conflict. Reuven experiences this conflict indirectly—as he helps Danny struggle through it, he struggles to understand it himself.

RISING ACTION

After Danny injures Reuven during a softball game, the two boys become friends and teach each other all sort of lessons. After many years, Danny's father, Reb Saunders, decides to end Danny's friendship with Reuven. Eventually the boys are permitted to become friends again. Reuven discovers that Danny has applied and been accepted to graduate programs in psychology, even though Reb Saunders expects Danny to take over the leadership of his Hasidic community.

CLIMAX

Using Reuven as a buffer through whom he can speak to his son, Reb Saunders confronts Danny. He asks his son about his plans and explains his reasons for treating Danny with silence for so many years.

FALLING ACTION

After Reb Saunders issues his approval of Danny's plans for psychology, Danny and Reuven leave and walk together in silence. Reuven and Danny graduate from Hirsch College, and Danny goes on to graduate school at Columbia University. Reuven says farewell to Danny.

THEMES

The importance of parallels to individual growth; silence as a path to the soul; the conflict between tradition and modernity; choosing versus being chosen

MOTIFS

Father-son relationships; perception; suffering

SYMBOLS

Eyes and eyeglasses; the Talmud

FORESHADOWING

Foreshadowing is prevalent throughout *The Chosen*. The warm silence between Reuven and Danny at the hospital foreshadows the positive side of Reb Saunders' silence. David Malter's comments to his son about the dangers of being a buffer foreshadow the uncomfortable role Reuven will play as a buffer between Danny and Reb Saunders. Danny's revelation that his father inherited his role as a tzaddik when his brother (Danny's uncle) abandoned the family dynasty foreshadows the fact that Reb Saunders will have a complex and perhaps sympathetic response to Danny's own situation.

STUDY QUESTIONS & ESSAY TOPICS

STUDY QUESTIONS

1. *How does Potok weave together personal and political events in his novel? How do politics and world events contribute to the novel's plot and character development?*

The historical setting of *The Chosen* includes the final years of World War II and the creation of the state of Israel in 1948. These political developments drive the novel's plot. Danny and Reuven's friendship, the novel's central subject, is predicated on major world historical events. In the first chapter, Reuven comments that he never would have met Danny if not for America's entry into World War II. Reuven explains that a growing patriotic awareness of the importance of athletics to the war effort led Danny and Reuven's community to begin its softball league.

One of the major conflicts in the novel is Reb Saunders's and David Malter's difference of opinion about the proper way to respond to the Holocaust. In response to the murder of six million Jews, Reb Saunders says it is God's will and that man can only wait for God to bring the Messiah. In contrast, David Malter believes that American Jews must give the Holocaust meaning by preserving the Jewish people and creating a homeland in Palestine. This fundamental difference of opinion between the two men ultimately drives Reb Saunders to end the friendship between Danny and Reuven.

Political developments are not just a backdrop to the novel; they motivate the novel's character and plot developments. Potok implies that in the modern world, individual lives are inseparable from larger historical developments. He also asserts that it is important for people to actively engage the outside world.

2.   *How does Potok use silence as a narrative technique?*

The epigraph to Book Two of *The Chosen* is a quotation from the Zohar that reads "Silence is good everywhere, except in connection with Torah." The Zohar is the central text of Kabbalistic knowledge (see the Glossary for an explanation), by which Reb Saunders raises his son Danny. In accordance with the teaching of the Zohar, Reb Saunders never speaks to Danny except when they are discussing the Torah. At the end of the novel, Reb Saunders explains that the purpose of this silence is to teach his son to have compassion in his soul.

However, silence is not only a defining aspect of the way in which Reb Saunders raises his son, but also an important aspect of Potok's writing style. Potok uses spare language. Characters often sit quietly, immersed in their own thoughts. Long pauses in conversation are found throughout the novel, even when the topic of conversation is silence itself. In the last scene of the novel, when Reuven's father asks Danny if he will raise his own son in silence, Potok writes, "Danny said nothing for a long time."

Often, a character says nothing in response to a statement about which he obviously has strong feelings. When Reuven learns that Danny has been teaching himself German, he is shocked. Even so, when Danny asks what is wrong, Reuven does not reply. Potok leaves gaps in his story and describes the characters' silences because he intends for us to have the same experience as his characters. As readers, we must fill in the gaps, just as Danny must listen to his father's silences and fill in the gaps. We must search within ourselves and within our understanding of human behavior to recognize what such pauses communicate.

Potok also uses silence in the novel's thematic development. He refuses to reveal the meaning of Reb Saunders's silence, creating a mysterious silence about silence that builds as the novel progresses. Like Reb Saunders's silence, Potok's silence forces us to examine more carefully the details Reuven relates—it leaves us with a deeper, more personal sense of Reuven and Danny's world.

QUESTIONS & ESSAYS

3.   *Discuss the meaning of the novel's title. Who or what is*
     chosen in the book? Which is more desirable: to be
     chosen or to make a choice?

The novel's title refers to the idea that the Jews are God's chosen
people and therefore hold special privileges and responsibilities.
Both Danny and Reuven fulfill their duty by studying Jewish liturgy,
and they derive great pleasure from Jewish traditions. At the same
time, both protagonists feel the burden of being Jewish—the burden
of being a member of a persecuted minority. Reuven is saddened by
the loss of lives during the Holocaust, and Danny struggles with the
Hasidic tradition he was born into. In its reference to Judaism, the
novel's title refers to something the characters have no control over.
This lack of control has both positive and negative effects on the
characters.

Danny struggles to choose his life path rather than have it chosen
for him. Danny is not only born into a religion; he is born into a very
demanding culture with a strict set of customs and expectations. To
Danny, being chosen is especially cumbersome, because his lifestyle
and education are limited by the rules of his culture. As a Hasid, he
cannot choose his wife, and as a tzaddik, he cannot choose his profession. Yet Danny nevertheless defies his father's expectations and
chooses another path, deciding to become a psychologist.

At the end of the novel, we learn that this path was in fact something Reb Saunders chose for Danny, when he made the decision to
raise Danny in silence. At the same time, Reb Saunders's method of
parenting was chosen for him—he raised Danny the only way he
knew. At the novel's conclusion, we see that creativity, spirituality,
and inspiration can emerge out of a situation in which one has no
choice. Potok's message is ambiguous. He shows us that being chosen has both positive and negative consequences; it has both
unpleasant obligations and rewarding privileges.

SUGGESTED ESSAY TOPICS

1. Many critics have written that THE CHOSEN *is a distinctly American novel. They argue that the novel's plot is centered on the concept of the American dream, the ideal that anyone can have the opportunity to become anything. Do you agree or disagree with this analysis? Could the novel take place in another setting?*

2. *Discuss Judaism in* THE CHOSEN. *Why are there no important non-Jewish characters? Why is the novel restricted to a Jewish environment?*

3. *In* THE CHOSEN, *every character, event, action, and idea seems to have a parallel, an opposite, or a complement. Identify several such relationships, and explain the purpose they serve in the novel.*

4. *Why do you think Potok chose to tell the story from Reuven's point of view? What narrative advantages does Reuven have over Danny? What advantages does Reuven's limited first-person perspective have over an omniscient third-person perspective?*

5. *Compare Reb Saunders's political ideology to David Malter's. At times, each father feels threatened by the other's views. At other times, each father displays strong respect for the other. How are the two men different from one another, and how are they are similar? How can they both dislike and respect one another at the same time?*

6. *Where are women in* THE CHOSEN? *How do they play a part in the story? If they are absent, why do you think Potok excluded women's voices?*

7. *Throughout the novel, Potok uses imagery of eyes, glasses, and other items associated with vision and perception. What do these images symbolize? Discuss several examples, including at least two in which eyes reveal a character's feelings.*

Review & Resources

Quiz

1.   What does Reuven's father want his son to become?

    A.   A doctor
    B.   A rabbi
    C.   A mathematics professor
    D.   A Hasid

2.   Which of the following characters is not hospitalized at some point in the novel?

    A.   Levi Saunders
    B.   Reb Saunders
    C.   Reuven Malter
    D.   David Malter

3.   Which of the following characters strongly supports the creation of the state of Israel?

    A.   Reb Saunders
    B.   David Malter
    C.   Levi Saunders
    D.   Mr. Galanter

4.   Which of the following historical events takes place during the novel?

    A.   End of World War II
    B.   End of World War I
    C.   Yom Kippur War
    D.   Vietnam War

5.   Who cooks meals for Reuven when he is at home?

    A.   His mother
    B.   His father
    C.   Manya
    D.   Mrs. Carpenter

6. What position does Reuven play most of the time on his softball team?

    A. First base
    B. Second base
    C. Third base
    D. Pitcher

7. Where does Danny go to graduate school?

    A. Harvard University
    B. Yeshiva University
    C. Columbia University
    D. University of California, Berkeley

8. Who recommends books to Danny in the library?

    A. David Malter
    B. Rav Gershenson
    C. Professor Appleman
    D. Mr. Merrit

9. What is Danny's critique of his psychology classes at Hirsch College?

    A. The material is too easy
    B. The material contradicts his religious beliefs
    C. The content is too scientific
    D. The classes make him feel inadequate

10. Why is Reb Saunders opposed to the creation of the state of Israel?

    A. He believes that Jews should wait until the Messiah arrives
    B. He thinks that Israel should be founded in South Africa instead
    C. He supports the Arabs who are against the creation of a Jewish homeland
    D. He does not believe that Jews need a homeland

11. Which of the following boys plays baseball on Danny's team?

    A.   Davey Cantor
    B.   Sidney Goldberg
    C.   Schwartzie
    D.   Dov Shlomowitz

12. How did Billy lose his eyesight?

    A.   He was born blind
    B.   In a car accident
    C.   In a fire
    D.   During an operation

13. Who is considered the founder of Hasidism?

    A.   Reb Saunders
    B.   The Ba'al Shem Tov
    C.   Solomon Maimon
    D.   Rabbi Abraham Gershon

14. Why does Reb Saunders raise Danny in silence?

    A.   He wants Danny to have a compassionate soul
    B.   He wants to make his own father proud
    C.   He thinks that silence will make his son a better psychologist
    D.   He feels that silence will make Danny focus on intellectual pursuits

15. Which of the following is true of Danny at the end of the novel?

    A.   He shaves his beard
    B.   He stops keeping kosher
    C.   He publicly insults his father
    D.   He goes to Israel

REVIEW & RESOURCES

16. What is the term for a person who opposes Hasidism?

    A. Mitnagdim
    B. Tzitzit
    C. Yeshiva
    D. Gematriya

17. Why must Danny listen closely to his father's
    Sabbath speeches?

    A. He is required to commit them to memory
    B. He is not allowed to take notes because it
       is the Sabbath
    C. He must be able to explain the speech to Reuven
    D. His father will quiz him on the speech afterward

18. Reuven excels in which of the following subjects?

    A. Logic and mathematics
    B. History and philosophy
    C. English and grammar
    D. Chemistry and physics

19. What language does Reb Saunders speak in conversation?

    A. German
    B. Hebrew
    C. Yiddish
    D. English

20. Where do Reuven and his father vacation in August?

    A. On the beach
    B. In a resort town
    C. In a country cottage
    D. In a private country club

21. When does Danny's father acknowledge that his son will not
    take his place as head of the dynasty?

    A. During Hanukkah
    B. During Passover
    C. One Shabbat afternoon
    D. On the day of Danny's graduation from college

REVIEW & RESOURCES

22. Which of the following Saunders family events does Reuven attend?

    A. Levi's Bar Mitzvah
    B. Danny's cousin's wedding
    C. Danny's grandfather's funeral
    D. Danny's sister's Bat Mitzvah

23. Which of the following subjects is Danny unable to teach himself?

    A. German
    B. Freud
    C. Talmud
    D. Symbolic logic

24. Reuven expresses a romantic interest in which of the following women?

    A. Manya
    B. Danny's sister
    C. Danny's cousin
    D. Rav Gershenson's daughter

25. Which of the following terms does not apply to Reb Saunders?

    A. Spiritual leader
    B. Tzaddik
    C. Hasid
    D. Zionist

REVIEW & RESOURCES

ANSWER KEY:

1: C; 2: B; 3: B; 4: A; 5: C; 6: B; 7: C; 8: A; 9: C; 10: A; 11: D; 12: B; 13: B; 14: A; 15: A; 16: A; 17: D; 18: A; 19: C; 20: C; 21: B; 22: A; 23: D; 24: B; 25: D

A GLOSSARY OF TERMS USED IN THE CHOSEN

Apikorsim A derogatory term for Jews educated in Judaism who deny the basic tenets of their faith.

Bar Mitzvah A ceremony that initiates a thirteen-year-old Jewish boy into his congregation and confers on him his religious duties and responsibilities.

Hasid A member of the Jewish mystical sect called Hasidism.

Hasidism A Jewish mystical sect founded in Poland around 1750. Originally, Hasidim honored spirituality and piety over rationalism and mechanical worship. Reb Saunders's brand of Hasidism, however, is less inclusive and open-minded.

Kabbalah Kabbalah refers to the tradition of Jewish mysticism, particularly the mysticism codified in the Zohar. But because "the Kabbalah" refers to not a single thing but a tradition (in fact, the Hebrew translation of "Kabbalah" is "that which is received," i.e., a tradition), it is a term that encompasses a broad range of beliefs and practices, and that is difficult to reduce to a single definition. Generally speaking, Kabbalistic thought teaches that the mysteries of God are all around us, always within us, and that the goal of religious study is to approach these mysteries and, in doing so, to understand better the mystical secrets of divine nature and of the world around us.

Kashruth A Hebrew word that literally means acceptable. Kashruth refers to food that conforms to kosher dietary laws.

Shabbat The Jewish Sabbath. Shabbat lasts from sunset Friday night until shortly after sunset on Saturday night. During this period, Jews are commanded to refrain from working and observe a day of rest.

REVIEW & RESOURCES

Shul   The Yiddish term for a house of prayer and study.

Smicha   Rabbinic ordination.

Talmud   An authoritative, holy text that contains a code of Jewish law (the Mishna) along with discussions about those laws that occurred among rabbis of the fourth and fifth centuries (the Gemara).

Tefillin   Also known as phylacteries, tefillin are two small leather boxes containing specific passages from the Bible (Exodus 13:1, Exodus 13:11, Deuteronomy 6:4–9, and Deuteronomy 11:13–21) written on parchment. As part of the traditional morning prayer ritual, Jews bind these boxes with thin leather straps to their head and left arm.

Torah   The Five Books of Moses, also known as the Pentateuch.

Tzaddik   A righteous Hasidic leader who is believed to be a superhuman link between man and God.

Tzitzit   Fringes of strings worn by religious Jewish males on the four corners of their garments to remind them of God's Commandments.

Yeshiva   A Jewish school and center of Torah study.

Zionism   An international movement supporting the establishment of a Jewish national or religious settlement in Palestine.

Zionist   A supporter of Zionism.

The Zohar   The central text of Kabbalistic knowledge (aside from the Bible), the Zohar is a compendium of mystic discourses dating, in written form, from the late thirteenth century.

SUGGESTIONS FOR FURTHER READING

ABRAMSON, EDWARD A. *Chaim Potok*. Boston: Twayne, 1986.

FIELD, LESLIE. "Chaim Potok and the Critics: Sampler From a
Consistent Spectrum." In Studies in American Jewish Literature.
Vol. 4. Albany: State University of New York Press, 1985.

KREMER, S. LILLIAN. "Chaim Potok." In Dictionary of Literary
Biography. Vol. 152. Detroit: Gale Research Inc., 1995.

ROSS, JEAN W. "Chaim Potok." In Contemporary Authors (New
Revision Series). Vol. 19. Detroit: Gale Research Inc., 1987.

STERNLICHT, SANFORD V. *Chaim Potok: a Critical Companion*.
Westport, Connecticut: Greenwood Press, 2000.

WALDEN, DANIEL, ED. *Conversations with Chaim Potok*. Jackson:
University Press of Mississippi, 2001.

WERBLOWSKY, DR. R. J. ZWI AND DR. GEOFFREY WIGODER, EDS.
The Encyclopedia of the Jewish Religion. New York: Holt,
Rinehart and Winston, 1965.

3 1143 00775 8569

SparkNotes
Test Preparation
Guides

The SparkNotes team figured it was time to cut standardized tests down to size. We've studied the tests for you, so that SparkNotes test prep guides are:

Smarter:
Packed with critical-thinking skills and test-taking strategies that will improve your score.

Better:
Fully up to date, covering all new features of the tests, with study tips on every type of question.

Faster:
Our books cover exactly what you need to know for the test. No more, no less.

SAT and PSAT are registered trademarks of the College Entrance Examination Board, which does not endorse these books.
ACT is a registered trademark of ACT, Inc. which neither sponsors nor endorses these books.

SparkNotes Literature Guides